EVERYDAY SACRED

Also by Sue Bender

Plain and Simple
Plain and Simple Journal
Plain and Simple Wisdom

Everyday Sacred

A WOMAN'S

JOURNEY

HOME

SUE BENDER

Illustrations by
Sue and Richard Bender

HarperSanFrancisco
An Imprint of HarperCollins*Publishers*

FIRST EDITION

ISBN 0–06–251289–7
ISBN 0–06–251290–0 (pbk)
Library of Congress Cataloging-in-Publication Data:
Bender, Sue.
    Everyday sacred: a woman's journey home / Sue Bender. — 1st ed.
    p. cm.
  1. Self-actualization (Psychology)—Case studies. 2. Holy, The—Case studies.
3. Bender, Sue. 4. Spiritual biography. I. Title.
BF637.S4B436 1995
291.4'092—dc20
[B]   95–14808

95 96 97 98 99 ❖ RRD(H) 10 9 8 7 6 5 4 3 2 1

CONTENTS

With love this book is dedicated to

Richard, Michael, and David

and

Mitzi McClosky

and

Laurie Snowden

We do not great things, we do only small things with great love.

—MOTHER TERESA

This story is about a bowl.

A bowl—waiting to be filled.

If what I have just written makes no sense to you,
I am not surprised.

If I had known in the beginning what I was looking for,
I would not have written this story.

I had to trust there was a reason I had to write,
and I didn't have to have it all figured out in order to begin.

I would find what I was looking for
along the way.

For as long as I can remember I have been listening to a harsh, critical voice inside me, but I've lived with it so long that I never really noticed the influence it was having on my life. I not only listened, I believed what this *harsh judge* was saying.

The voice passes judgment on *everything* I do.

"You're not measuring up!" the judge shouts.

I'm never sure what I am supposed to measure up to, only that I never will.

Nothing I do will ever be enough.

"Don't complain," the judge adds, "you have it easy."

Judging myself harshly for having a harsh judge only makes matters worse. When I try to ignore it, the voice gets louder.

I could have read all the books in the world about showing "loving kindness toward oneself," but I could do nothing to stop the voice of the judge.

I felt a hunger inside that I didn't understand and couldn't satisfy.

Miracles come after a lot of hard work.

That was the last line of my first book, *Plain and Simple*. It was the story of a journey that led me to live with the Amish.

Everyday Sacred is the story of another journey, a journey to learn about the sacred in my own life.

My need to learn was connected to the harsh judge, but I didn't understand the connection until I had almost completed this book. Not everyone has a harsh judge, but many of us have some inner voice that has the power to undercut, to make us doubt ourselves—and leaves us wondering why we aren't more content.

To begin to make every day sacred, I first had to step back and look at the judge—and everything else in my life.

Maybe I wrote *Everyday Sacred* to learn more about miracles.

HOW IT BEGAN

"I'll never write another word," I thought with relief when *Plain and Simple* was published. I felt complete—exhausted and satisfied.

I had survived an obsessive love affair that had taken over my life for seven years. Cross out person and put in project: the feeling was the same. I'd felt the excitement of going overboard—a fierce single-minded intention, none of it making sense—and I believed I had no other choice.

Now I had a choice.

I would come home and calm down. I would do one thing at a time. I would work in my studio with clay, something I loved doing. I wouldn't rush. I would live the simple life I had learned about among the Amish—calm and purposeful.

"Art is order, made out of the chaos of life," Saul Bellow once wrote. I scribbled the words in pencil on a scrap of torn paper, placed it on the white Formica table next to my bed, and held it down with a large pewter heart.

I expected my life to be transformed.

I expected a miracle.

At first my days were unhurried. I enjoyed whatever I was doing. The spirit of the Amish was all around. On those days I felt grateful.

Then, hardly noticing it, I started getting busy, saying "yes" to the many things that were offered. Suddenly I had too much on my plate. I had slipped back into an old groove, frantically scurrying to get everything done, crossing things off a never-ending list, and feeling the constant weight of all that was left undone.

I was back in the world of *"never enough."*

I still felt a hunger inside that I didn't understand and couldn't satisfy.

"You should have called your book *Hectic and Chaotic*!" my son David observed.

I had learned a lot, but not enough.

The day I heard that *Plain and Simple* had made the *New York Times* best-seller list I happened to meet a good friend at the vegetable store. Glowing, I told her the remarkable news. It seemed like a miracle.

"What number are you?" she asked, her voice showing neither delight nor wonder.

For a moment, I didn't even know what she was asking.

Then I realized she wanted to know what position I had on the list. That was one of those moments when everything stops and a space opens up. In that instant I could see that in this world nothing I did would *ever* be enough.

I was still anxious. I was fifty-eight years old and did not want to spend my remaining years feeling this way. Something was still missing, something *more* that I should be doing so I could feel good about myself and the life I was leading. Even this achievement, far beyond anything I had ever expected or dreamed possible, could not silence that critical voice.

EVERYDAY SACRED appeared one day in my mind's eye, in sure, bold letters, like one of those blinking restaurant signs. I didn't even know what everyday sacred meant, but I knew it would be the title of my next book.

Two years went by and I didn't write a word.

Then on a day when I was feeling particularly discouraged, another clear image appeared:

A BEGGING BOWL.

Actually, it reappeared.

I had read M. C. Richards's *Centering* years before. It was a book about clay and art and life. In it, Richards described Jean Genet, the French playwright, who had said he wanted to roam the countryside like a monk, holding a begging bowl, having filled it with what he needed for the nourishment in his life.

EVERYDAY SACRED and now the BEGGING BOWL.

It was obvious to all who knew me that I wasn't a monk, and the very idea of begging would make most of us uncomfortable. In spite of that, the image of a begging bowl reached out and grabbed my heart.

The image of the bowl became the image of the book.

All I knew about a begging bowl was that each day a monk goes out with his empty bowl in his hands. Whatever is placed in the bowl will be his nourishment for the day.

I didn't know whether I was the monk or the bowl or the things that would fill the bowl, or all three, but I trusted the words and the image completely.

At that moment I felt most like the empty bowl, waiting to be filled.

I turned on the computer, hoping to write, but no words came. With the computer still humming, I walked, practically galloped downstairs to the studio and opened a twenty-five-pound bag of clay, ready to make my first begging bowl. The moment my hands touched the clay, I remembered a wise and wonderful statement that M.C. Richards had made many years ago:

"It's not pots we are forming, it's ourselves."

Like the monk going out with his empty bowl, I set out to see what each day offered.

I began noticing, the way an observer might, what I was doing —all my thoughts, feelings, and experiences that might be connected to *everyday sacred*.

Somehow, in some way not yet shown to me, I felt there was a connection between EVERYDAY SACRED and the BEGGING BOWL.

I looked up *sacred* in the dictionary and found: "entitled to reverence." Close by was *sacrament*: "a practice that is considered especially sacred as a sign or symbol of a deeper reality."

Are ordinary, familiar things "entitled to reverence"?

I wanted to *see* with fresh eyes.

What might have been there all along that I had not been able to see? What had I taken for granted?

When I began looking, I found teachers everywhere. Some were officially designated "wise people." Others were not, but were equally wise. Memories from the past reappeared, fresh. Objects reached out with lessons to teach.

I learned from everything and everybody.

What follows are the *stories,* the *people,* and the *experiences* that filled my bowl—a connect-the-dots record of my search for the sacred in everyday life.

OUR BOWLS, OURSELVES

I had hoped to find a straight path. Instead, my path led in circles. I wondered how I could write about my journey if the path led in circles? How would I find *order*? Then I found these beautiful words in Deena Metzger's *Writing for Your Life*. She was quoting members of A Traveling Jewish Theater.

"Stories move in circles.

They don't go in straight lines. So it helps if you listen in circles. There are stories inside stories and stories between stories, and finding your way through them is as easy and as hard as finding your way home.

And part of the finding is the getting lost.

And when you're lost, you start to look around and to listen."

Perhaps it was no accident that the begging bowl had reached out and caught my attention. Bowls have always intrigued me. Everywhere in my house, in every room, in every corner, are bowls I have made.

Three months before our first son, Michael, was born, I stopped working. For the first time in my life I had free time and signed up for a ceramics class. I loved being with clay. Touching clay felt like a way to come home to myself. I started making simple bowls by hand and found that, after a while, I could do it on "automatic." The bowl would appear as if by accident. No conscious plan and no struggle.

For the last thirty-four years every single bowl I have made has been crooked.

When one accidentally comes out symmetrical, I instinctively whack it out of shape. Though the forms are simple and hand-made and direct, no two are the same. Each has a spirit all its own.

The designs are geometric, black on white clay, sometimes with the mythical animals and people of an early Native American culture. Sometimes I add a dash of red.

For me the bowls (whether I use them as bowls, pots, or cups) are much more than utilitarian. They take care of my spirit.

The bowls are my "family."

A bowl, whatever its shape, is open. Open for possibilities.

STORY OF THREE BOWLS

I heard a story about three bowls.

The first bowl is inverted, upside down, so that nothing can go into it. Anything poured into this bowl spills off.

The second bowl is right-side up, but stained and cracked and filled with debris. Anything put into this bowl gets polluted by the residue or leaks out through the cracks.

The third bowl is clean. Without cracks or holes, this bowl represents a state of mind ready to receive and hold whatever is poured into it.

Sometimes I am that first bowl, so busy being "productive" that I don't notice when the very thing I want presents itself. Sometimes I am the second bowl, with such a fierce judging voice that focuses on what's *not* working that I'm unable to see or appreciate all the things that are going well.

And sometimes, wonderful times, I am the third bowl, able to be present and absorbed in what I am doing, whatever it is.

AN IMPERFECTLY PERFECT BOWL

Long before I started thinking about begging bowls and everyday sacred, I saw a strikingly handsome Japanese tea bowl that had been broken and pieced together. The image of that bowl made a lasting impression. Instead of trying to hide the flaws, the cracks were emphasized—filled with silver. The bowl was even more precious after it had been mended.

When I first read about Genet and his begging bowl I was leading a group I called *Warriors of the Spirit*. None of the women in the group had worked in clay, and many resisted when I told them that we'd be making begging bowls.

"I can't do that! I'm not an artist," the women protested, almost in unison, as if they too might have been listening to harsh judges. I knew that if they could suspend judgment, not care so much what the bowl looked like, they might discover something new about themselves—a glimmer of what was in the deepest place in their heart.

I asked,
What do you *need* in your bowl?
What do you *want* in your bowl?

At the time, I did not understand that the essential practice of a monk is to *accept* what is placed in his bowl—and be grateful.

"It's not pots we are forming, it's ourselves," I said, reminding them of M. C. Richards's words.

EMPTY

I was giving a talk one day to a group of quilters. Quilters love slides. I am awkward around machinery and don't have a friendly relationship with slides. By chance, that morning I opened the slide box and found nothing there. Just the empty tray.

"I am empty," I said, stunned—startled by the truth of that statement.

OVERFLOWING TEA

Over time I've read five books that have told five slightly different versions of the same story. I call it *Overflowing Tea*. The setting changes but the cast of characters remains the same: there's always a wise Zen monk (or hermit), living in a remote place, and an earnest student who has made a pilgrimage to see him, traveling a long distance to find his teacher.

The student arrives seeking wisdom.

The serious student, his head filled with questions, is annoyed and becomes more and more frustrated when his teacher refuses to answer his questions.

"Pour me a cup of tea," the monk eventually says, "and I will tell you when to stop." The dutiful student starts pouring the tea—and pouring and pouring the tea. The bowl fills and he is horrified, watching as the tea finally spills out of the cup and over everything. Exasperated, the student finds the courage to speak.

"Can't you see the cup is full? It can hold no more!"

"And so it is with you," the wise teacher answers. "Your mind is full of too many things. Only when you are empty will there be room for more knowledge to come in."

"I am empty" no longer seemed a doomed prophecy.

I would begin with an empty bowl.

STARTING

I visited a friend and saw on her wall strong and powerful Japanese calligraphy written on beautiful handmade paper. "What does it say?" I had asked, struck by its beauty.

EACH STEP IS THE PLACE TO LEARN.

GALE'S POT

By indirections find directions out.

—William Shakespeare

One evening, needing a ride to see a friend who was in town from Japan, I was given the name of a woman named Gale who was also planning to go. I called and she offered me a ride. As Gale said goodnight to her six-month-old twin sons, I looked at the drawings on her wall: round, fat, voluptuous, sensuous, luscious-looking pots, in pastels that burst with vitality and joy.

It was in fact the same pot, done each time in different, intense colors and combinations.

"How did this pot find its way into your life?" I asked Gale several days later.

"It was just around, part of the surroundings in a studio I rented," she said, "always in the corner of my eye. Just the kind of shape I liked, fat and simple." A white metallic enamel pot, fourteen inches wide and nine inches high.

Gale had been in the studio seven years when a fire destroyed nine-tenths of her work. Cleaning up afterwards she had trouble parting with the most unlikely things—an old wood stool she used to stand on and the pot! She asked the owner of the studio if she could have the pot. "Sure, take it. It has no magic for me!" The pot went with her to a new studio in Berkeley and became the receptacle for cleaning utensils.

19

Gale was also teaching a graduate art class called *The 100 Drawings Project*. The task of the class was to find and draw one hundred times, one simple, familiar object, portable enough to bring to class each time. It had to be neutral in content, not religious, not a family heirloom, nor an object that held any sentimental attachment. After hearing Gale describe the assignment to the first class, one of her students asked if she had done this project herself. She hadn't, and decided to join the class in the homework.

Looking around her environment Gale spotted the pot! She stared at it and felt the pot observing her. "Take me off the shelf," it seemed to say. "It tells you, rather than you telling it," was her description of the transaction. Her first four black-and-white drawings were made easily, quickly, with little attachment to the outcome. Then, with ninety-six more to do, and later with fifty more, Gale had exhausted all known possibilities and didn't know what to do.

Knowing nothing about photography, she began taking pictures of the pot in different circumstances. She noticed that its white enamel surface could reflect anything; it acted as a *mirror,* taking on the qualities of its surroundings. She experimented. At midnight she went out to photograph the pot using the car's lights to illuminate it. The headlights created a dramatic black-and-white contrast; brake lights turned the pot red; hazard lights produced a yellow pot. Sitting next to the TV, the pot turned blue.

As Gale experimented, she became more and more interested in color. She thought about the pot's original function. She put the pot on the stove and boiled water in it. Silhouetted against other dark pots, a golden glow in the background produced the quality of a seventeenth-century Chardin painting. Over time her drawings became very real, intensely photorealistic.

She took the pot with her in a knapsack on a European vacation. Wanting to capture the colors of Italian cities, she photographed the pot in Florence where the stones reflected ochre and mustard and beige on the pot's surface. Rome produced a deeper, dark yellow and ochre, and a pink cast found its way onto the pot in Bologna. Reflections of the many tiny colored lights at night by the water's edge at Piazza San Marco were captured on the pot's surface. The pot visited and had its picture taken underneath Michelangelo's tomb in Santa Croce, in Florence, and on a niche outside the cathedral at Chartres.

"Sometimes I'd find the simple, unassuming little place would be more remarkable than the remarkable place," Gale told me.

Sitting down at a fountain to rest and think about where to photograph next, she'd turn around and there—just where the pot was sitting, resting—was the perfect place to photograph it. "Chance settings were often the magic settings."

Making one hundred drawings of the same object forced Gale to find new techniques, materials, and ways to work. The goal here was to take risks and exceed limits. Hopefully, along the way, a personal style would emerge.

I spent a lot of time daydreaming about Gale's pot.

The pot led many lives: utilitarian object, icon, travel companion, and mirror. There's something universal about a simple pot. Gale's pot didn't have any innate drama or significance. Working for hours, day after day, she was able to take this most ordinary object and imbue it with meaning.

What struck me was that if you can take a white enamel household pot and begin seeing it brand new each time, *you can do it with anything.* If there are one hundred ways to see an ordinary white pot, imagine all the possibilities for viewing with fresh eyes an "average" child, an "average" marriage.

Gale was telling me a story about *relationships.*

Each time, the pot was just being the pot, but at the same time it reflected everything that was around it. It was Gale's ability to be present to *see,* really see—to recognize the sacred in this seemingly mundane pot—that made the difference.

"I don't look at objects the same way anymore," Gale said.

"Objects have begun to look back at me. Any object can have a magical quality. When I'm drawing I don't want to be anywhere else but right there, doing that drawing in that moment."

One day I asked Gale, "Were there any surprises?"

"Yes," she said. "When the project was finished, I realized that it didn't matter where I was drawing or what I was drawing—whether it was a landscape or still life or an object—the same quality came through. Everything I drew conveyed a quality—a feeling of waiting—expectation. Something about to happen."

Eventually Gale realized the choice to draw her pot wasn't all that neutral. This pot, a survivor of the fire, was also a metaphor for her body, her belly. The pot was always drawn empty—waiting to be filled. For some time she had been longing to have children. Each one of those one hundred drawings was a self-portrait.

"Now look what's happened," she added. "Twins!"

CHERI'S X-RAY BOWL

At my friend Cheri's studio I saw beautiful abstract photographic prints that were both haunting and powerful. When I asked what created the rich and poetic images she told me she used discarded X-rays of people and animals—transforming "useless" objects into art.

That evening she knocked on my door. "I didn't know if you'd want this?" she said, handing me something flat wrapped in plain brown paper. When I opened it, there was a perfectly formed elegant bowl staring at me. "What is it?" I wanted to know. "It's so beautiful."

"An X-ray of the sacrum and pelvis of a woman."

Sacrum comes from the word sacred. My sons, I thought, emerged from a wondrous bowl.

SEARCHING FOR ORDER

One afternoon I bumped into my friend Mel, a Zen priest, dressed in blue jeans and a plaid shirt, looking very much like everyone else shopping for vegetables at our neighborhood market.

He asked how I was, and I told him about the *Overflowing Tea* story I had written that morning.

"That's me," I said.

Before he had a chance to answer, I added, "And the image of my new project is a begging bowl. Can you tell me anything about begging bowls?"

"Oryoki," he said (the Japanese name for a begging bowl) "means 'just enough.'"

JUST ENOUGH.

Two words.

Somewhere between the image of an empty bowl that made me feel peaceful and the too much that was driving me crazy, was a moderate, balanced space of JUST ENOUGH.

What is the path from *Too much* to *Just enough*? I began to wonder.

After living with the Amish, I thought I might stop making lists, but I still make them—lists even the most effective person could not make a dent in. I sit down for a half hour early each morning to write all the things I hope to do that day, letting myself believe I can do it all.

There's a connection between my lists and the piles of paper that cover every usable surface in my room. "The piles are winning the war," I told my friend Yvonne one day. "No matter how hard I work, I don't seem to make a dent in them." Earlier that morning an important piece of paper had been mislaid; I had rifled through the piles, becoming more and more harried, finally panicking. "How could this happen?" my judging mind demanded.

"This morning," I tell her emphatically, "is a metaphor for my life."

"It's not a metaphor for your life," she said calmly. "This *is* your life."

If I had a *wish* list, high on that list would be to have ORDER in my life.

"Whoever knows how to organize his life can be comfortable anywhere, even in hell!" I once read. I'm not sure that is true, but I keep on in the belief that an ordered house will create an ordered mind.

Someone walking into my home would probably be struck by the order and calm and beauty of the house. What they cannot see is the hidden mess. Upstairs, out of sight, are the twelve white file cabinets bulging with files, all labeled, but with no system or "sorting principle." Really important things are put away in a "special place" and are impossible to find.

I do not want to spend my life making a mess and then cleaning it up.

These incomplete tasks weigh on me—my mind often focuses on what I'm *not* getting done rather than on what I am doing.

Desperate to be rescued from the overload of paperwork, I hired a professional organizer. After an hour and a half I asked if I could pay her extra to leave. Eager as I was to have help, I resisted her every suggestion. She meant well; what I resisted was her way of making order. One day I'll find an expert willing to hear my peculiarities and honor my attachments to certain pieces of paper as *part* of the solution.

I first read the words "creative ordering" in *She,* a book by Robert Johnson. I smiled, delighted. Adding the word *creative* to something I find difficult—my endless, losing battle to make order in my life—allowed for new possibilities.

I came up with a plan, made a contract with myself that seemed sensible and doable. I would spend one hour a day SORTING. It didn't matter which room, drawer, cabinet, closet, or file I picked. One hour. The only rule was that while I was doing whatever I'd chosen to do, I would not spend any good energy noticing how many hours, months, years it might take to get all the other projects finished.

The first day I tackled all the jars, prescriptions, razors, perfume, and shampoo in the cabinet under the bathroom sink. The next day four bookshelves in the bedroom were the focus of my attention. Some books were put in a pile to be given away, the rest sorted into categories.

I was surprised by how pleasurable these small tasks were.

They were of manageable size. Manageable and doable.

Having a limited time frame, and without rushing, I was able to approach each job with focused attention. Filling and emptying a big straw wastebasket created a rhythm that was satisfying. That one hour, no matter what else I had chosen to do that day, was as sweet and satisfying as anything I could have imagined doing.

Before, trying to make order had been hateful. Now I look forward to my one hour of *homework* and the completion of small tasks.

FROM THE BOTTOM UP!

I was visiting a remote Zen temple on the southern Japanese island of Kyushu, twelve hours by bullet train from Tokyo; a place with no electricity, phone, or TV—and no car.

Ekai, my monk friend lives there. He has a beaming open face with a shiny shaven head and the clear, electric eyes of someone who has done a lot of letting go and a lot of zazen sitting. He spoke of his pleasure, the challenging tasks: training the monks, supervising the building of a new temple on the grounds, the outreach to the community, and once a month, the ritual of going to the small town nearby to beg. He described how life was organized for the seven monks from Japan and the two from a Zen center in Minnesota.

They get up when it is still dark, about 3:00 A.M., and meditate until they hear the first birds sing. At night they begin their meditation just as it gets dark.

Three months ago, a local supporter of the temple, hoping to make life easier, had given the community a gift, a small minivan. Before the arrival of the van the monks had a simple schedule. Several times a week they walked down the steep mountain to a small village outpost where they waited for the bus that would take them into town. There they bought supplies and fresh vegetables, just what they could carry on their backs, and then retraced their path up the mountain. A balanced life of possibilities and limits.

"How are you and how are things going at the temple?" I asked Ekai on the third day of the visit, when we had a moment alone.

"Wonderful and hard," Ekai said. "I feel the car is running me. Now I seem to go up and down the mountain too many times. There is even *more* to do—too much," he shrugged.

"I love to work in the kitchen," he said, with a sweet smile on his face.

"Lately, I've been so busy with all this new work around the car, I can see that the kitchen isn't working." And then he sighed, and added, "Life doesn't work when the kitchen doesn't work. From the bottom up."

KEYS IN THE KITCHEN

The dictionary says, "*order*: a system of regular arrangement."

Placing two keys, one for the house and one for the car, on the very same spot on the kitchen counter every time I come into the house may not sound like a very large accomplishment, but it is for me. I have spent too much of my time searching for important things.

As I write the words *two keys,* I see for the first time that having only two keys is one way my life *is* uncluttered. And what I do each day with the two keys creates a very modest, but successful ritual. The repetition is something I can count on.

I long to accomplish a great and noble task, but it is my chief duty to accomplish small tasks as if they were great and noble.

—Helen Keller

Today I have thirteen things on my to-do list and I give them all equal weight. Even working hard I know I will only be able to do three. "What should I do?" I asked a friend, "I'm drowning in possibilities."

"Do more of less."

She is right. First, shifting my focus from what isn't working to what *is*—and then doing a little bit and feeling satisfied are wonderful feelings.

"What you do may seem insignificant, but it is very important that you do it," Mahatma Gandhi said.

A BRILLIANT IDEA

On my sixtieth birthday someone gave me a book by
Marguerite Duras. She was writing about *disorder*, and
I was struck by her quote saying:

"Get rid of things or you'll spend your whole life tidying up."

One day a friend suggested that I put away everything in the
room where I'm writing: all the piles of paper on the floor and
on the tables and on the shelves. I had just read a review of a
book about Albert Schweitzer's life and read "—a clearing in
the woods—cutting out from the thicket to make way for the
sun."

That's what I would do—make way for the sun.

The idea of walking into this room and not being flooded with
sensory overload—all the visible evidence of possibilities—
thrilled me.

The truth was I was not ready to throw the papers out. But I
could certainly manage to put them in a closet and *shut the
door*. Doing the best I could for the moment was *more* than
enough. It was a triumph.

"What's happened?" my son David asked the next day. "The
room is so different."

I postponed writing as long as I could. I had talks to give, workshops to lead, a book tour to go on. And then there was the paperwork. I could always count on the paperwork. Finally I set a date. Whatever wasn't done by that time would just have to wait.

On the last day before my deadline I decided to clean my desk, which is really just a large wooden door painted white. Not one inch of white was showing.

Everything went on the floor.

I stared at the new empty white space.

It looked luscious and peaceful. Slowly, tentatively, I put back a few beloved objects: a homemade crooked black and white ceramic cup filled with pens, pencils, and scissors; one white file case, supposedly to hold the really important files; a few postcards of the Buddha sent by friends, each with a serene expression; a phone; a small TV; and two officious-looking rolodex files that I've never learned to use but was told are useful if you want to be orderly. All the rest I moved slightly out of sight.

My desk became still, a still-life composition.

Many months later I found I still hadn't used those rolodexes, and moved them to a place on the floor. The empty space they left seems gigantic.

TIME AS A TEACHER

Why are there times when I don't know, and it doesn't seem to matter, and times when not knowing fills me with dread?

"To suffer one's confusion is the first step in healing," I read.

I was relieved.

CAPPUCCINO

Early every morning I go to a café near the Berkeley campus, Cafe Milano, to make my list for the day, write, and have a cappuccino. After talking to Gale I found myself looking into my cup of cappuccino, seeing it as if for the first time.

Martin, from Guanajuato, Mexico, is there making the cappuccino. No matter how long the line, he never seems to rush. He has a quality I've read about in books but have rarely experienced—"a still point in the midst of activity." As he is about to hand over each drink, he stops, and with a gentle flourish, makes a smiling face in the foam.

That gesture is the opening ceremony of my day.

Being greeted by a different smiling face each day has become a *sacred* ritual.

Martin is shy, and in this situation I am also shy. We hardly talk, but his act of generosity blesses my day.

A couple of years ago a friend of mine fell off a bike during vacation and hurt her knee. She and her husband were going on a hike in a national park and she could only walk very slowly.

She discovered her slowed pace helped her look at the world as if through a microscope.

As they walked along so slowly, she discovered a lizard that was in the process of devouring a centipede. They spent ten minutes watching. The centipede was trying to sting the lizard, but the lizard knew just how to avoid that. "Of course I would have missed this if I hadn't hurt my knee."

Right behind them there was a single hiker with a big camera. Every time my friend stopped to examine a wildflower, he would stop and look at the wildflower too—as if she were discovering something for him. Finally the hiker came up to her and said,

"You're seeing so many wonderful things."

"I'm seeing these wonderful things," she told him, "because I can't walk very fast."

OFFERINGS

One day I went to visit Mel to ask him more about *offerings*.

"In many religious traditions a monk sets out with his begging bowl and an exchange is made," he began. "Food is placed in his bowl and he accepts the offering gratefully. The offering gives him strength to do his work and, in return, he gives guidance and wisdom. Who gives? Who receives? Both are giving and receiving."

"What does a monk do when he's feeling deluged?" I asked.

"The monk puts his bowl away when he is finished eating," he answered. "If he ate all the time, there would be no time to digest."

"Even when I am doing things I enjoy," I tell Mel, "I don't leave time to digest or savor what is happening. I almost never pause before going on to the next 'doing.'"

"Put a lid on the bowl," he said with the smile of a sphinx.

"How do I walk around with a bowl that is overflowing?" the driven seeker wanted to know, unable to stop asking questions even after receiving the answer I needed.

"You walk very carefully."

"What are you doing?" the flight attendant asked, genuinely curious as I cut and pasted small pieces of paper from a very large pile.

"I'm writing a book: this very large pile of papers is the *Introduction*. When I'm finished it will be two pages."

"I used to do circles," the flight attendant responded, sounding quite pleased with herself. Then she explained, "Before, I ran around in circles." This was a delightful surprise. I hadn't said a word about circles, or told her about the image of the bowl, which I see as a circle.

"I used to be really inefficient," she continued, "but I'm a single mother, and now, besides my job as a stewardess, I have an extra job selling cosmetics. I've learned to make lists: go to the post office, go to the bank, *order my priorities*. I'm more focused and know what I'm doing. Now, when I get up in the morning, it's one part of the circle. And at the end of the day I complete the circle."

Another container. A day is a circle.

PRACTICING PATIENCE

When I described this encounter with the flight attendant to my friend Mitzi she suggested that some people look at life as a pie—with a limited number of slices. She imagines many pies, or the pie expanding to include each new necessity. Mitzi has learned to *phase things in*.

Knowing that anything she really cares about will get done, she began her Ph.D. at age twenty-two and completed it when she was fifty-five. Now in her seventies, she's writing her first book. "I never would have begun this book if I had had to squeeze it into a limited time frame."

When I think about my days, almost any day, I think about not having enough time. But Mitzi's small shift made me see that even if I can't do everything at once, I can do many of the things I want if I am willing to give them space and time and patience.

LESSONS FROM A SMALL ITALIAN TOWN

Two hours after my husband and I had arrived in the small Italian town, I wondered why I had come. Normally I would have loved to be there, but this time, though I wasn't able to say it out loud, I had been reluctant to abandon my writing schedule at home.

My first hours in town were spent wondering how to escape. Then Richard developed a cold and a terrible hacking cough, and I would have felt like a rat if I had left immediately.

I remembered Mitzi, normally resilient and optimistic, telling me of the time she and her husband went to live and work in New York for two years. Their apartment was on 56th Street between Lexington and Third Avenues—an intensely crowded and commercial neighborhood. She hated the noisy streets, and the scale of the city made her lose her sense of place.

Eventually she carved out a two-block area around her apartment—getting to know the shoemaker and shopkeepers, creating a small island of calm in the midst of all that she couldn't control.

These two blocks became her sanctuary.

She enjoyed venturing beyond, knowing she could return to a place that now felt like home. Mitzi's shift from "something-is-going-wrong" to "this-is-what-has-been-placed-in-my-bowl" turned a potentially unhappy situation into a challenge for her—and an inspiration for me.

The first thing I did was re-create my early morning cappuccino ritual in this small town in Italy. Finding a place to have a good cappuccino and write for an hour wasn't difficult in a town that had a café on every street. I knew I couldn't re-create my life in Berkeley, but a rhythm developed, and I worked diligently.

Though I still carried in my wallet the basic information about what it would cost and how long it would take to get back on the plane, the chance that I'd use this information got slimmer and slimmer.

I arrived back in the States with a few stories, eight extra pounds, and a very stiff neck. "On a scale of one to ten for stiffness, your neck is a ten!" my physical therapist told me. I had been so determined to reframe a problem into an opportunity that I had spent too many hours poring over a tiny computer screen in my hotel room—not paying attention to what my body needed. Nothing I did helped to get rid of the stiffness.

"You did what most of us do when we're stressed," Mitzi said kindly.

"You self-correct in the wrong direction."

She was right. Even when my computer breaks down and registers *overload*—with warning signals and blinking lights—I never think to stop and relax for a while. I smile and say "Yes, a message from the Universe"—and push myself twice as hard.

Resting when exhausted was never on my list of possibilities.

Resting when exhausted is now on my list of possibilities.

LITTLE SABBATHS

"We all need a certain amount of fallow time," Yvonne reminds me.

"*Watching the grass grow,* sitting on the hillside, staring out the window daydreaming. When we don't have it, there is a deeper intelligence that won't come forth."

Mine is a racehorse rhythm, and once I get started in the morning it's difficult for me to stop. Now I can see that a pause—even a very *small pause*—is extremely useful.

These "little Sabbaths" replenish my body—and spirit.

TIME

I remembered how everyone laughed and looked puzzled when they heard that Richard and I had chosen to take a twelve-hour train ride on the bullet train in Japan to visit Ekai. Flying would have gotten us there in an hour and a half. "We should start a bank for all the time people save," Richard said with a smile.

During our stay with Ekai at his mountain monastery, he told us how for years the local farmers would come to visit the temple after a long, hard day of work. Because they had no cars, and the trail up to the temple was steep, they would arrive shortly before dark. The monks and the farmers would spend happy hours chatting together by the fire and then the farmers would sleep at the temple.

Now each farmer has his own small car and there is no longer time for this leisurely visit.

NOTHING IS WASTED TIME

This week I inherited Richard's old computer. Delighted with the possibilities, I cleaned the work table, lined up hundreds of old discs in an orderly fashion and, in the process, cleared my mind. *CREATIVE ORDER* was my topic.

The computer proceeded to go haywire: first the screen went blank, then dancing, wavy lines appeared, and finally strange hieroglyphics.

How quickly calm disappears.

Stunned, too agitated to continue working, I sat down at my desk, took out a piece of paper and pen, and started having a dialogue with the computer.

Me: Why did you have a temper tantrum? I did everything I could to insure a good start.

Computer: You think there's a magic rule you can count on to make things go smoothly. Things will always happen *beyond* your control.

What a relief. "Things will always happen *beyond* your control."

Of course, on one level I know that. But I often don't act as if I know.

When circumstances can't be changed, *I* can change.

I can learn from obstacles placed on the path. Now, when I feel particularly stuck and think something is definitely going wrong and start believing the judge, I remember the computer blowout and the lesson I learned.

Nothing is wasted time.

If I can learn from a mistake, then it is not wasted time.

The only mistake is to not learn from a mistake.

One day, in search of something else, I found a book called *Wabi Sabi*. *Wabi sabi* are the Japanese words for a feeling, an aesthetic that is hard to describe. I read:

"Wabi sabi is a beauty of things imperfect, impermanent, and incomplete.

It is a beauty of things modest and humble.

It is a beauty of things unconventional."

A friend, a student of the Japanese tea ceremony, mentioned "October tea." She said it's one of the most important times of the year for tea, the most wabi. November celebrates the new tea, but October is the time to use up the last of the old. Instead of letting it dribble out, or be thought of as the dregs—"We cherish what remains of that which is in the process of passing."

This month only, mismatched dishes are used. The utensils are ones that have been broken and repaired. "Not just repaired, but carefully and beautifully mended," she added.

When I began to look at my day the way an observer might, when I relaxed and didn't try to force anything to be "interesting," I was surprised at what I saw.

My day begins at 4:30 or 5:00 A.M.

I'm not sure if that's a natural rhythm or a conscious choice I made thirty-four years ago when my sons were one and almost two years old. In those days I found that by getting up even half an hour earlier I could make a cup of coffee, read the *New York Times,* and have a little time to myself before the demands of the day and small children took over. Now I realize that may have been my first attempt to carve out "sacred" time.

My day begins slowly.

Before skimming the newspaper, I read one page in each of three small "inspirational" books. The books change, but they are always ones that remind me that I am not alone, that there is a spirit larger than myself at work, a universe larger than my immediate self-interest and concerns.

Several years ago I hurt my neck by not paying attention to my body, and a doctor suggested that I stand under a hot shower to loosen the muscles in my neck before going out for a walk or exercise. No one suggested I end the shower standing under ice cold water, but I decided that was a good idea. The rush of cold certainly is a jolt and gets me to take a deep breath—another morning ritual.

Each morning is a new day—a fresh start.

I used to leave the house at 6:20 A.M. to get to an aerobics class which begins at 6:45. Once I actually left at 6:28 and got there on time. Yesterday, I had to make a phone call to New York and didn't get into the car till 6:35. I drove, anxious, with a terrible feeling of scarcity. There wasn't going to be enough time.

Time for what? I wondered.

I arrived *just* in time.

What's the lesson?

Do those extra moments add anything to my life?

WHITE WALLS

Today when I went into the bathroom at Cafe Milano, instead of the usual lurid graffiti, I found white walls. It must have taken six coats of paint to cover the written and graphic explosion that had been there for two years. The change was dramatic and soothing. White walls and a very clean, rust-colored Mexican tile floor.

Fresh paint, fresh start.

Are these white walls going to be a temptation, I wondered? How long will it take until the walls are covered again?

Twenty-four hours later I found one small graffiti.

"Bathroom graffiti is the only form of democracy."

My artist's sensibility questioned why, with three blank walls, this unknown writer/artist had chosen that particular spot, off in a corner.

"There's a difference between freedom and democracy, Bozos!" appeared the next day.

The management attempted to discourage this new dialogue by whitewashing the two sayings. But they could still be read if you really stared hard.

"Nothing lasts forever. Deal with it!" arrived on the third day.

IMPERMANENCE

Yesterday, a week after my annual mammogram, came a dramatic wake-up call: "We've noticed a dark spot on your left breast. We want you to come in today."

I know nobody lives forever. But I don't ordinarily include impermanence, a word that has such a cool distant ring to it, in my list of possibilities. Suddenly it was very present in my thinking.

Today I sat in a cold, antiseptic room with a large X-ray machine that had just squeezed my breast, waiting for Diane, the technician, to consult the expert. There was no place to hide. "This has been placed in my bowl *right now,*" I thought. "I cannot say, 'No, I don't want it. Take it back. I prefer something else.'"

Do I have to hear dramatic bad news in order to change? What if they say the spot is O.K.? Will I immediately go back to *not* thinking about these things? Happily, the report was fine.

To celebrate I cleaned the house.

RICHARD GETS SMARTER

Many years ago, when our sons were quite young, my husband had a sabbatical year and the family went to Europe for six months. "Do you have a research grant? Are you going to write a book?" well-meaning friends asked.

When Richard said "no" to all these questions, our friends looked worried. We took the boys out of school for the year and meandered around places we had always wanted to visit, and I remember the pleasure of sharing wonderful places with them and also of being able to be flexible.

No appointments to be kept. No schedules to conform to.

Nights when we were all tired we ate at 5:00 P.M. and then went to bed. Other nights, when it felt right, we took a nap and went to dinner at a time when most Europeans ate.

We stayed places until we felt like leaving, having no rooms booked ahead, no plan. It created a relaxed, easy time and I was struck by the difference it made. When we returned to America we put the boys' bikes on the top of the VW and drove at a leisurely pace across America, heading to Berkeley, where Richard would teach for six months. When we arrived I noticed that Richard, who is very bright, seemed to have gotten much smarter.

"Don't just do something. Sit there," I once read.

If stopping and allowing a pause worked magic, why did we not continue to do that? We had come upon a really useful piece of information, why did we spend the next twenty years going at our old hectic pace?

Why is "not doing" so hard?

OBJECTS AS TEACHERS

When I told Gale I wanted to write about her and her one hundred pots she said, "Fine." Then she added, "It's just an ordinary pot! My work is about ordinary objects as they simply are."

But Gale brought something to that pot, a quality of attention that inspired me to look at my day and the objects around me with fresh eyes.

I'm not comfortable talking about my strengths, but there is one thing I know I am good at. I have a talent, an instinct for finding what teaches me. Even when what I need presents itself in the most unlikely form.

MOROCCAN BOWL

Many years ago my husband and I were in a small village in Morocco, high in the Atlas Mountains. While checking into the hotel I noticed on the counter an unglazed, soft orange, voluptuous pot, with two rakish handles, filled with flowers.

It was a glorious sight.

Its simple rounded monochromatic form contrasted with the splurge of colored flowers. Each day I looked at the bowl and was struck by its beauty. Usually I'm a disciplined traveler and am rarely tempted to take anything home, but this was an exception. I coveted this bowl.

On the fifth day I asked the man at the desk if I could buy the bowl. "No problem," he said. "There are a hundred more just like this one in a shop near the square." I was delighted and immediately set out to purchase my own bowl. He was right and he was wrong. There were indeed about a hundred similar unglazed pots with the same form—and not one had that certain extra something—I want to call it soul. None would have tempted me to carry such a fragile piece home.

When I returned to the hotel I told the manager what I had seen. "Could I buy *that* pot?" I asked, pointing to the bowl at the counter?

"Of course," he said. "It makes no difference. They're all the same."

BOWLS, BOWLS, BOWLS

One day Yvonne and I sat around talking about bowls. Images of bowls and real bowls filled the room.

"Bowls that are bells, bowls made out of human skulls, bowls that are made into drums," she began. "There are the bowls that native people make—handsome baskets, so tightly woven that they could hold soup or porridge; old American Indian funeral pots made with holes at the bottom to let the spirit come through.

"There are summer bowls, Zen tea bowls from Japan, used in the tea ceremony, that have a wide brim to help the heat of the tea escape, and winter bowls with brims that are made narrow to hold in the heat when the weather is cold. And big brass water pots that the women of Rajasthan carry on their heads."

I told her about an honored old Korean bowl I saw, also used for tea ceremonies, made with poor clay and even worse glaze. Over time, water and tea stains had developed under the glaze. This kind of ever-changing bowl is called "rain spotted" because the bowls remind them of the leaks that often come into the tea house in the rain.

"Physicists even see the universe as a bowl," I added.

If you start being curious about bowls you begin to see them everywhere.

GREGOR'S TABLECLOTH

A friend told me about the "home" he had when he lived in Europe during World War II. The family, his mother and younger brother, moved constantly from place to place, from hotel to inn to a friend's home and back to a hotel again. Each time they would arrive, his mother would open the small suitcase filled with all their belongings and bring out the lace tablecloth that she had used for the Friday night meal in their home in Poland, before they were forced to leave and begin their travels.

In each place the ritual was exactly the same.

She would place the suitcase on a table, carefully drape the tablecloth over the suitcase, light a candle, and in that moment, the place, wherever it was, became HOME.

EKAI'S RAKUSU

My friend Ekai is a Japanese Zen monk. I went to visit him at the San Francisco Zen Center when he was in town for a brief visit. The first thing I noticed was a rectangular piece of material resting on his chest, something like a bib, about twelve by nine inches, held on by a two-inch-wide piece that went around his neck. The material was made up of pieces of dark-colored cloth; browns, rust, deep, deep purple held together by tiny white running stitches. "Ekai, that small garment around your neck is beautiful. It reminds me of a very old Amish quilt fragment."

"Take it," he said.

I was startled. "No, I can't," I exclaimed. We then proceeded to go through a back-and-forth dance—"yes-no,"—and in the midst of my vehement protesting, I realized I'd love to have it, I wanted it badly would be more accurate. "Yes, I'd love it," I finally said, at last telling the truth.

I had what I wanted and felt guilty.

Flooded with misgivings, I told myself I had no business taking it. I'd been so busy *wanting* that I didn't know I wasn't supposed to take it. And my friend was just too polite to tell me the truth. I'm not a Zen student, but if I were, I told myself, I would have eventually made one for myself. On and on I judged myself, but I was unwilling to give back the gift.

So now I had it. I accepted that, and with that acceptance came a deep sense of responsibility—for what, I did not know.

Ekai's rakusu became a talisman.

I gave to it qualities I thought I didn't have and would put it on at special times. Sometimes I wore it when I had to talk on the phone to my editor and defend the vision I had for the book.

Anyone from the outside, looking in, might have thought it strange that this worn, tattered piece of material could be so sacred to me. Sometimes when I needed courage, but didn't feel I could wear it on the outside, I would fold it carefully in my bag so it would be nearby, protecting me.

I was later told that in the Buddhist tradition a rakusu *is* a sacred object.

When I was asked to go on a ten-city book tour for my last book, the first thing I planned to pack was the rakusu: it would protect me. When it was time for my first radio interview in Denver, I opened my bag and searched everywhere but couldn't find the rakusu. I had been so excited, so fearful. I had wanted to shine. I collapsed in tears under the weight of all that wanting. I thought of the poet Rilke saying, "To succeed is fine. To long for success is bad."

"What am I supposed to learn from this?"

I sobbed, standing in my hotel room. Messages don't always come on demand, but this time, perhaps because I was feeling desperate, the words were clear and calming. "You have to take the qualities you saw in Ekai's gift, the qualities you think are outside yourself, and bring them inside."

That intervention helped me get through the ten days of the tour. Many weeks later, back home in Berkeley, I found the rakusu in one of those "safe places" we put things that are especially important.

ZUNI FETISH

Audrey, a friend, owned and treasured a rare Zuni fetish, a carved onyx wolf sitting in the "singing position," with its head raised towards the moon. To honor a friend of hers at a critical time, Audrey lent her the wolf.

Her friend assumed it was a gift and Audrey did not have the heart to say, "No. This is mine. I need her!" When Audrey was next in Santa Fe, she went back to the shop where she had bought her wolf and asked for another just like it. A customer, overhearing her, came up and said, "Maybe you don't need it anymore. Perhaps your wolf had done whatever she could for you."

Something had been completed—rather than lost.

WHITE PAINTINGS

Absolute certainty is not in my normal vocabulary.

On a trip to New York my husband and I went to see the reno-vated warehouse that had become the downtown Guggenheim Museum.

The uncluttered long white exhibition space floated—a limitless expanse of calm and stillness. I was not prepared for the beauty of the white walls. And on the walls were white paintings. White walls, white paintings. Placed at intervals were four or five Brancusi sculptures. That was all. My heart was pounding. This was what a temple should feel like: a "temple of the soul."

Many people moved around, looking. Were any of them as affected as I was? Would we know, looking at each other, that we had something in common? Or were they bemused, trying to understand why anyone would bother to paint white pictures?

I had not heard of Robert Ryman, the artist of the white paint-ings, so I placed myself next to a guide leading a group of art students, hoping to learn more. "Why waste all that space on someone who doesn't show anything?" someone asked. "It makes me feel empty," another added. "I don't know why the director chose these paintings for his opening show!" The guide agreed. I listened. I felt no need to disagree. At that moment I understood that each of us in that room was bringing our own meaning to the white paintings.

An "inner light" radiated from the paintings.

The space was silent—with that respectful, muffled silence of a cloister. The word *purity* came to mind.

And immense.

This was the "immensity within ourselves" I had read about and hadn't understood.

"It doesn't always have to be so hard," I heard myself say—the judge nowhere present at that moment. There are other ways of "seeing"—these paintings seemed to say. Other possibilities, infinite possibilities. Mysteries to be uncovered.

SERENDIPITY

This is how I first met Yvonne Rand. I heard about a class given by a lay Zen priest. The announcement read, "Can we integrate the 'monk' in each of us with our ordinary life in the world?" Although I'm not a Buddhist, I thought, This is what I need.

The class was full, and the term already half over when I called to ask if I could join. Yvonne said, "Come, and introduce yourself afterwards."

After class I stood patiently in line. The woman ahead of me asked for an appointment, and Yvonne took out a large black book and penciled in the time and date. When the woman realized she could not make it on that particular day, I had to control the urge to burst in and say, *"I'll take the appointment."* I had no idea what the appointment was for—therapy, spiritual guidance—and it made no difference.

When my turn came, my rational mind took over and I realized I didn't know what I would be asking for. I said a quick, civilized "hello" and walked away. The following morning I awoke feeling intensely incomplete. I wrote Yvonne immediately, "I want that appointment!"

The appointment was for 9:00 A.M. at her home, which is on the other side of Mt. Tamalpais, about an hour's drive from my home in Berkeley—on a good day. Because I am compulsively on time, and terrible at directions, I set out very early with my map in hand in pelting rain and gray dense fog.

All went well until I made a turnoff for Stinson Beach. I had been on those roads before, so I knew my destination was quite

close; I read the signs, and went in the wrong direction. High in the mountains, the winding roads dangerously narrow, in the fog and the pouring rain, with no one to ask, and no place to turn back, I kept on in what I feared was the wrong direction.

An inn at the high point of the mountain confirmed that this was not my route, but one headed in the opposite direction. A woman gave me directions and I set out, a bit more relaxed because she was clear and had said "When you get back to the crossroads—*Go straight!*" I found my way back to the intersection, but there was no "straight," only left or right.

I began to imagine myself in the mountain clouds of Tibet or the Himalayas needing a guide. Finally, I saw a truck parked on the side of the road, but all the driver could say was, "This is a terrible map!"

Here was a perfect metaphor of my life. Was I on the right path?

I went back to the intersection, made two more false starts, turned around both times, and finally committed to one direction. When I got to the Pelican Inn, clearly marked on the now drenched map, I knew I was only five minutes away and could still get to my appointment on time. But her address was not on any of the small, muddy country signs in the vicinity.

Could every choice be wrong?

I gave a pleading honk when I saw a woman, a forest ranger. She offered, "It's a small community and I can't tell from this map, but follow me." After a few passes she pointed to a sign that was Yvonne's address. "I've made it," I thought with relief, and fifteen minutes early. At three minutes to 9:00 A.M. I walked out into the deluge, thinking her house was right there by the side of the road behind some tall hedges.

Torrential would not be overly dramatic to describe the rain that was falling on me. No house. Eventually I saw a small wooden gate, went through it, and knocked on the door to a house. No answer. I knocked harder. "Yvonne, it's Sue. I'm here!" Still no answer. I shouted, almost screamed, "Yvonne, let me in." By now this compulsively on-time person was late, fighting back tears.

I walked farther down the lane to a house with many cars outside, banged on the door, and was greeted by a woman with a kind face. "Please, I'm looking for Yvonne and I can't find her. I know she must be very near." "Yes," she said, "her house is just around the corner." She started giving directions. "Please, take me to the house," I said. She smiled, got her umbrella, and led me there.

Yvonne, heavyset, walked with a very light step. She took my totally soaked shoes and leaned them up against the fireplace. Probably everything I needed to know had already transpired on that three hour journey.

But I was still eager to begin our "appointment." She wanted me to meet her "family." In five minutes I met the most eclectic collection of devils, demons, saints, and sacred objects I had ever seen in one place, coexisting quite happily.

We sat down in a small, cozy room to talk. I still didn't know what kind of appointment this was, and I didn't ask. Maybe all the rain and all the mistaken paths had exhausted my thinking mind. I plunged in, telling her about *Everyday Sacred,* the bowl, my confusion. Why did I feel compelled to write this book? Can I write from a place of not knowing?

Can a "path of the heart" feel so uncertain?

"The image of the book is a begging bowl," I continued, intent on telling her that although I trust the image, I don't have any rituals that involve a bowl. "Is there a modest practice I might begin?" I wanted a practice so modest that I wouldn't get discouraged and give up. She said something that was not clear to me at the time, because I think the excitement of getting to my "appointment," and the pleasure of being there, had clouded my thinking mind. Nevertheless, what she said made a huge impression.

I heard the word *generosity*.

And then something about what the bowl sees—and something about noticing what comes my way. "In the Buddhist tradition, *generosity* is the ground for everything else," she said.

It didn't matter that I had just begun making the begging bowl in form, it was already there in spirit. I had been working on it in my heart for a long time.

The possibility that I could begin by placing generosity in my bowl meant I could practice generosity toward myself and to others, and I could take a breath of fresh air from being so hard on myself.

I could begin a generosity practice, and see where it would lead.

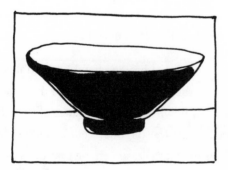

EXPECTATIONS

A few years after *Plain and Simple* was published, the publisher called to say they had decided to send me on a book tour. I was thrilled. I had spent several years saying "yes" every time I was invited to give a talk. Now the publisher would do the organizing and I would only have to do what I liked best: feel the connection with an audience, telling them things I myself needed to hear.

One month before the tour I panicked. My tongue erupted in a moonscape of bumps that weren't canker sores, and, though the dentist wasn't sure what they were, it hurt every time my tongue touched my teeth. "Alligator's Tongue" I called it. Paralyzed with fear, I imagined standing mute in front of the audience.

In desperation, for the first time in my life, I went to a hypnotist.

The story I told her was an old-fashioned melodrama—a battle for my soul between good and evil—between the gentle, stoic, wholesome values of the Amish and the striving, driven, competitive New Yorker. "Pick me!" each side shouted. The stalemate was sapping my energy.

The hypnotist listened.

"Sue, you have the soul of the Amish—and the blood of a New Yorker!" she said.

What she said had such a ring of truth to it that I stopped in the middle of my sad story and laughed.

Her words changed something that had been unacceptable into something that could be tolerated. The hideous "alligator's tongue" unearthed treasures. The "blood of a New Yorker," which I had been rejecting, was also a source of strength, allowing me to *persist* in the face of problems that in the past would have discouraged me enough to turn away from the project.

I *was* a driven seeker.

Without that driven part I would never have set out on a quest. I would not have found the Amish, begun looking at what I really valued.

The "alligator's tongue" had burst out from wanting *more*.

In wanting to give an even better speech than I had ever given, in never being satisfied, I was making myself sick. I had crossed the fine line between wanting a challenge and overreaching.

I hadn't learned that doing the best I can do is different from being THE BEST.

Today I write with a bellyache.

Proud of an ironclad stomach, I'd often said I could match any-one in my ability to survive the hottest of hot food in any coun-try. I don't get bellyaches. My stress leaks out in sinus infections and an exotic variety of rashes—dots, spots, blotches, and red-colored markings. On this particular Sunday I hobbled to Cafe Milano and ordered hot water, feeling at age sixty that I was experiencing birth pains.

"Why am I feeling this way?" I asked myself.

The answer came quickly.

My son Michael, who likes to be called *Bender*, had come home for a month. This was a really unusual event for all of us in the family. He was thirty-four and he had been away for the last ten years becoming a dedicated, compassionate pediatrician. Seattle isn't all that far away, but it's rare for him to have more than two days in a row when he's "off." When we do get to see him the time feels precious, and I was anxious, hoping it would be a good visit.

Our last, brief visit was difficult.

The first night had gone well. The next morning we drove in the rain up to a small town outside of Seattle, and I could feel the mood in the car switching. Michael was getting that "look" that says, "Why are you being that way?" What I hear is,

"Why can't you be a better mother?"

How did we get in this mess?

This dance is so familiar that it's hard to notice exactly what triggers the upset. We two, who do indeed love and admire each other and are very much alike, manage to get into this "snit" after being together a short time—even though we BOTH want the visit to go well.

And once we're into "it," it's hard to get out. That day, no matter what I said, hoping to make things better, the mood in the car got worse. Finally I gave up and withdrew. "O.K., if whatever I say bothers him, I'll keep quiet." For me that is not easy.

Hurt and defensive, I said to myself, "If this is what it takes for my son to be able to be with me—me having to sit on my feelings—it's not worth it! I don't want to be around anyone who doesn't like the way I am—or how I act—even if it is a person I love."

I can't remember exactly what I said to get things turned around. It had something to do with telling the truth—how hard this was for both of us. The rest of the brief visit went well.

Now Michael was home for a month to do a residency at Children's Hospital in Oakland. Given more time, could I learn to be the mother he would like me to be? Could we find ways to be together without bumping heads? Could we learn another dance?

I did something ridiculously intrusive that first morning—knowing it was ridiculous, and continuing to do it anyway.

By 10:00 A.M. the pain in my stomach had arrived.

My first attempt at rebirthing a child—improving a relationship that is dear to me—was having a bumpy beginning.

The absurdity of my behavior that first day must have released something in me because I relaxed and Michael relaxed and we laughed at the situation. I didn't have to make this month together a test. I could just be content that he was there.

"I need my ducks all in a row," a friend said, as I tried to describe this visit with my son. "I'm really not happy unless all my ducks are in a row. Fat little ducks filled with the things you expect to make you happy."

"Fat little ducks full of expectations."

What a wonderful image. My "pictures" of the way things *should* be between a mother and a son were my fat little ducks—full of expectations.

"Expectations become definitions," she added.

As the days went by I began to give up my pictures of what a good mother-son relationship was supposed to be. I had envisioned long, soulful, in-depth conversations, initiated by Michael—about his work, his relationship with his girlfriend Harriet, his thoughts about having children, and his long-term goals. A daunting list!

Michael's idea of a good time was to stretch out on our bed with the TV on, having a little light conversation, sometimes showing us some of the one thousand beautiful pictures of his trip to the National Park in Utah with Harriet.

Again, I'm not sure what happened to get me out of the old and entrenched groove, but this time, the judge out of the way, I enjoyed him exactly the way he was. Nights when Richard was busy, Michael and I tested a variety of inexpensive Chinese restaurants in the neighborhood.

"Don't try for perfection," my friend Mitzi suggested. "Trying to be good enough will be plenty."

I was getting my first lessons at "Good Enough" parenting.

The small shift in my expectations allowed me to accept that which at another moment would have been unacceptable. There was no sense of loss in lowering, even letting go of some old expectations. Just the opposite. I actively chose to make a small shift, and the results of that shift made me very happy.

The days flew by. Nothing dramatic to report. Michael was sweet and "easy," and we were all genuinely sad to see him go. When he called from Seattle to say he had arrived home safely, I could hear in his voice a new tenderness. Or, perhaps that tenderness had always been there. The difference was I'd always been so busy, distracted by the chatter of the harsh judge and a world of expectation, that I could not hear the sweetness.

Each of us understood this time together had been special. We didn't have to figure out why this difference happened— we could feel it.

LISTENING

Michael had always been an outstanding student. When he was eleven I stopped worrying about him in the work department. I knew he'd be good at whatever he wanted to do.

Two years ago Michael began expressing some of his concerns. He felt he didn't have enough medical information—a "fund of knowledge" he said it was called. Each time Richard and I heard his worry, we rushed in and reassured him.

"You're just being hard on yourself," we would say.

And it was easy to say these words because we totally believed it.

We didn't have to listen. We "knew" we were right.

Michael may be a perfectionist. It runs in the family. But that's not the point. We weren't listening. We couldn't hear his concern.

Michael was telling us something that was painful to him and our well-meaning but misguided validation wasn't helping him.

"To really listen you need a certain amount of relaxation and ease," a friend said. The minute she said that I realized that often I'm so busy asking questions, or getting ready to speak, that I can't hear what *is* being said.

I began to listen.

Listening to my children, without judgment, became one of my goals.

MICHAEL'S RESPONSE

I sent Michael a copy of what I'd written about him and us. I wanted to know his view of what happened.

"It's not so!" were his first words.

"I don't feel that way. I don't say to myself 'Why can't you be a better mother?' That's *not* what you hear coming from me." Then he continued, "What bothers me is this picture you present of the wonderful woman who has a problem son and she can fix him up!"

As I listen to Michael I realize there's always a risk when you ask someone to tell you what he or she is thinking or feeling. It's clear that Michael also has spent time and care thinking about our "dance."

"*We* got it turned around," he continued.

"We go through this *together*. You didn't do it all by yourself. We get in this together and *we* get out of it together."

He's not sure what the first step is, but it "starts small and grows."

"I'm ill at ease, not angry," he states. "Actually, *I'm* afraid I won't measure up to your expectations." Then he adds, "We can't be together for fifteen minutes without your commenting about my clothing!"

I am trying to listen carefully, respectfully. Michael is right. I work hard trying to do this mother-son dance right, but my fat little ducks filled with the things I expect to make me happy set me up to be disappointed.

"How would you like it to be?" I ask.

His answer is clear and comes quickly. "I'd like to be able to come home and have you relax with my just being there— instead of worrying about what 'magic' food from my childhood to get.

"I don't feel you should be a different or better kind of mother. I never think, 'Boy, I'd like her to be more of *that* kind!' "

"Don't you wish I were different?" my harsh judge asks, unable to hear the sweetness of what he has just said.

"I'd like it if you could relax more when we're together," he repeats.

Thank you, Michael, for being my teacher.

TELLING THE TRUTH

Several months after this visit with Michael, I went to New Harmony, Indiana, a remarkably beautiful, small town built in the nineteenth century as a utopian dream. I was invited to give a talk and workshop to fifty women artists who had gathered from all parts of the country.

When the workshop was over a woman in her seventies, conservative in dress and demeanor, raised her hand and spoke in a very quiet, refined voice.

"I said, 'No,' " she began.

"I've always done things for other people," she continued, "even when I didn't want to. But this time when they asked me to help out at the church benefit I said 'NO!' "

Every single woman in the room understood. She was telling us something that was important to her and wanted us to hear her discovery.

"I've done enough for others," she continued. "Now I'm going to do something for myself."

She had made one large decision. She was determined to shrink her list of "*shoulds.*" The one thing she was prepared to willingly do was listen, really *listen* when she was with another person.

Her face broke out into a huge smile. That smile filled the large room.

"When people started thanking me for what I had done for them, I was surprised. I hadn't done anything!" Later, she realized her "*just listening*" had meant a lot to them.

William Shirer said of Gandhi: "You felt you were the only person in the room, that he had all the time in the world for you."

"Listening is love," Yvonne said.

AIKIDO

When I was six years old, my well-meaning mother signed me up for ballet. While the other children seemed to know right from left instinctively, I was always headed in the wrong direction. The embarrassment was lasting. Almost never, if I could possibly avoid it, have I put myself in a place where I have to know my left foot from my right.

Recently a friend urged me to take an Aikido class taught by a wiry young woman with a fourth degree black belt. After ten minutes I was once again that inadequate six-year-old. I was planning my escape when the instructor stopped giving us physical instructions and began talking about how our bodies react to situations in ways unknown to our thinking selves. Later, she gave us exercises that let us see our patterns more clearly.

One day each of us had to stand in the middle of the room, while the rest of the class, one after another, came up and gave us a push—not the kind that would knock you to the ground, but strong enough so you lost your balance.

Our task was to come back to our center with both feet on the floor.

Standing there as a steady stream of "the other" came toward me, I had the physical sensation of what it's like to be grounded one moment, off balance the next. My picture of myself as a grounded person, standing rock-like, unaffected by the forces around me, vanished.

Just when I've got my whole life together I get another shove—
a reminder of how much I do not know and how much I am
not in charge.

AEROBICS CLASS

Going to an early morning aerobics class almost every day is a
testament to my willingness to be embarrassed.

There's a sweetness in surrendering to something I will never be
good at, and still finding pleasure in doing it.

Looking awkward doesn't seem as important as it used to.

WISHING

During the five years it took for me to write *Plain and Simple,* I
had to keep reminding myself EVERY day not to spend time
wishing I could write like Joan Didion.

Recently I was in New York for an American Booksellers
Association convention and a friend introduced me to Joan
Didion. I told her that story. "And I always wish I could write
like Henry James," she said.

When it was time to turn the manuscript for this book over to my agent, I couldn't let go. I made three honest attempts, each time sending it to her Federal Express, then calling the next day to say, "No. Wait. I have a little more to work on."

I wanted the manuscript to be wonderful and kept forgetting my own message—that things don't have to be perfect to be wonderful. Striving for some imaginary perfection also makes me miss what *is* there. A large, deep purple, bruise-like mark appeared on my chin. Like the alligator's tongue, it was a reminder: when I push myself to do something better than I am able to do at the time—my body collapses.

"Sue, haven't you tortured yourself enough?" my agent asked kindly.

My challenge was not to do the impossible—but to learn to live with the possible.

"The best of what we are is more than enough." Mitzi assured me.

THE PUPIL AS TEACHER

My brother's friend called from the East Coast to say she had just heard from her daughter that I would be in Oregon to give a talk to the Women's Press Association. "It would be a great help to me if you could find some time to spend with her," she said. "Be her therapist," she added. I had never met her daughter, but learned she was in her twenties, talented and intelligent, but her mother still worried that she was having trouble "finding herself."

We did meet. She came to the talk and after the formal part a small group got together to ask more questions about my writing process. Though writing is the best way I've found so far to look at my life and tell the truth, I still cannot see myself as a writer. This young woman listened and then raised her hand.

"Sue, I don't think it is wise for you to be so hard on yourself," she began. "Each time you say something critical about yourself you are making that message to yourself more real." This wise young woman, supposedly in need of my assistance, told me something very true.

How we speak to ourselves can have a powerful effect on what happens in our lives.

Sometimes the pupil is the teacher.

"Your interest in begging bowls is fine," my harsh judge says, prodding me, "and to find pleasure in small things is also fine. But you're not coming up with *big* conclusions."

"Doubt if you must," I tell myself daily, "but persist."

I might never have even recognized that I had a harsh judge, or understood her power to demolish my spirit, if friends had not shown their concern. "Why are you so hard on yourself?" they kept asking. The judge was even more powerful before I was consciously aware of her. Not only did I listen, I believed what she was saying.

When I finally realized the price I was paying for this deep-seated habit, I decided to get rid of her.

So much for wishing.

Her voice got louder and more insistent. Nothing I did made a dent in her fierce persistence. On a sunny weekend in June I spent two days indoors, in a rather stuffy room, taking a workshop given by Yvonne, called THE JUDGE.

"The first step is to *notice*," Yvonne began. "Don't try to change your behavior."

"Get to really *know* the judge. Notice the subtle ways she undermines your sincere efforts. Notice without blaming.

"We can't heal what we don't know.

"Treat her with a light touch," she suggested. " 'Oh, you're here again.' Start with a five-pound weight, not five hundred pounds! Show kindness to that critical voice," Yvonne concluded. "See how the judge serves you."

I left the workshop understanding that the judge would never disappear, but I could have a new relationship with this part of myself that I had wished would go away in a puff of smoke.

One day when the critical voice was particularly fierce, I took a pencil and paper and sat down and scribbled in large bold letters:

I WRITE BECAUSE I AM DESPERATE. THERE IS NO OTHER REASON.

I had labeled the judge "the enemy."

I discovered she was also an ally and a very good teacher. On some level not known to me when I began, she has propelled me to go on this journey. She fueled this search.

When I am desperate enough, the judge makes me hungry for my heart.

ESOTERIC BOWL

I heard about an ancient Buddhist teaching, an "esoteric bowl" practice, that at first sounded rather gruesome. A goddess, a terrific and fierce woman, wears a necklace of fifty freshly severed heads, and a crown with skulls on it. At her heart the goddess holds an offering bowl made from a skull.

The instruction for the practice is to visualize holding this skull in your left hand and a knife with a large handle and a curved blade in the shape of a nut chopper in your right hand. Next you visualize putting your worst thoughts and feelings in that bowl—anger, fear, feelings of being overwhelmed, hurt, shame, anything at all. Sweet and tender feelings are also placed in the bowl.

Next you use this "knife of wisdom" to chop up all your harsh, dreadful, disgusting aspects along with your tender aspects. Blending the negative and positive makes it easier to transform them into a proper offering—into nectar, ambrosia—a much richer brew.

This is a purification ritual, a rite of renewal.

Perhaps my "shadow" side is as fierce as that warrior goddess.

Perhaps I can imagine holding a bowl like this close to my heart and then symbolically placing my judge in the bowl and all the other unloved and neglected parts of myself that I wish weren't there, and all the parts that I don't want to admit are there. I can then chop and chop and chop till they are gradually transformed into an offering.

SUFFICIENT

SUFFICIENT

Yvonne has a gardener, a Mayan Indian from Chiapas, whose name is Aloush. He comes two days a week, works effectively but quickly, and knows a lot about plants. "I learn a lot from working with him," she told me one day. "I also like working with him because he's very quiet."

Yvonne and Aloush eat lunch together. Aloush eats a modest amount, which always amazes her because he works very hard. At the end of the meal he says,

"*Sufficient*, Yvonne, it is sufficient."

And the way he says sufficient is convincing and there is also a boundary about it. She is not to insist by putting more food on the plate or badger him to eat more lunch.

"It is sufficient."

A PERFECT MOMENT

On the day of their marriage, Yvonne and her husband were given a rare and gorgeous antique Hopi vase. After the ceremony someone carried the vase on a tray with too many other things, and dropped it. The bowl broke into many pieces.

"A perfect moment," she smiled. "The bowl was only whole for the ceremony."

92

Yvonne, Aloush, and three friends spent three days weeding a strawberry patch. They lifted all the strawberry plants out of the ground because many had gotten old, then carefully weeded the ground. Replanting them was a very big job. "A month later," Yvonne said, "if you looked at the patch you wouldn't say 'Oh, that's a strawberry patch.' You'd say 'Oh, that's a weed patch.'"

When Aloush arrived for work Yvonne suggested a complicated and time-consuming plan to attack the weeds again. Aloush listened, and then calmly shook his head and said "No. I don't think so." He suggested a modest plan. "If I pull the weeds carefully three or four more times, then they will be gone."

He spent the day quietly working with one tool, a machete, prying the weeds loose, and in a matter of hours he'd weeded a very big bed perfectly.

At lunch time Yvonne urged him to take a rest. "What I'm doing is not really hard work," he stated. "It is careful work."

"When Aloush is working on a bed of flowers he doesn't move around much; he digs a very big hole, and then puts the manure and dirt through a sieve. He puts a tremendous amount of energy into making beautiful soil.

"He's present in a way that's startling," Yvonne said, "His attention is what people aspire to when they do meditation practice."

DAVID'S TRUCK

My son David is one of those strong silent types. He lives in Berkeley and is a gardener. He keeps his tools in our garage. Today he mentioned that he was going to wash his truck, a task he does in front of our house. "But it's so clean," I thought. "What's he going to do?"

David's truck is ten years old; he's had it for four years and it looks brand new. He cleans it once a week, inside and out, and by the unhurried way he washes the truck, it's clear that he enjoys this routine. "Why do you keep the truck so clean?" I asked today. "Tomorrow it will get dirty again, especially if you have a hauling job."

"When I bought the truck, it was in really good shape," he answered. "The guy that owned it before me kept it immaculate. So I sort of inherited that same practice. I just enjoy keeping it in top condition. Right now, I'm coming up to 100,000 miles so I've been extra good about maintenance. Hopefully, I won't have to rebuild the engine or anything, if I just keep it up."

"Watching you wash your truck," I told David, "I felt I was witnessing an act of devotion, certainly not a chore."

"I'm not sure what devotion means," he said shaking his head, "but I do think it sort of reflects that my business is in order when I have a clean, well-conditioned truck. It says something about me."

David's connection with his truck, his sense of pace and attention, the way he has of caring for the things he uses, made me think of a line from the poet Rilke:

"When a poet rubs a piece of furniture," Rilke said, "when he puts a little fragrant wax on his table with the woolen cloth, he registers this object officially as a member of the human household."

David is one of my teachers.

MARTIN

When I told Martin, who makes cappuccino at Cafe Milano, that I was writing a book and had included him, he was surprised and pleased. I asked if he would talk to me about his work. During his ten o'clock break, he came upstairs to my table and we talked.

Martin started as a busboy in 1983. Angel, who was the cappuccino maker at the time taught him how to make coffee. "I learned a lot from Angel," he said with respect. When Angel left to go to another coffee house, he left Martin in charge.

"How did the tradition of making smiling faces in the foam get started?" I asked.

"Angel started doing it first. Angel used a little stick or a paper clip, and then one day he thought about using a spoon—and everything opened up." It's much easier to make clear, strong images with a spoon.

"I think people love to see your smiling face in the foam." I told him.

"Sometimes, even when it's very busy, I take a little extra time to make the face. It's beautiful for people. If I see them happy, I feel happy."

I asked him why cappuccino tastes so different when it's made by different people using the same machine and same coffee. Martin smiled. "Everything has to be perfect. There's this extra touch; you have to pack the coffee in a little tighter, there's a little more strain. Some coffeemakers don't want to bother. It's really important to press the coffee just right. I always put a little more effort into it. Sometimes I don't make the coffee right. It's hard to make foam with low fat milk."

"Can you feel how much your customers like you?"

"The customers are very important to me.

"Work is very important for me," he continues. "I think people appreciate what I have done. A little more trouble and extra work is good. When I'm in a bad mood, I hide it."

He mentioned the word "humble." I asked what it means for him.

"I don't want to take advantage. I don't want money. I want something . . . " and then he paused. "Something *inside,* more than money or material things."

Martin grew up on a farm in Guanajuato, Mexico, with his grandfather. His grandfather was serious, quiet, extremely honest. "Maybe I inherited some of that. He's guiding me, the way I behave. Poor but happy, proud."

Aloush, David when he's washing his truck and doing his gardening, Gale drawing her pot, Martin making cappuccino—each models a way of being present. They aren't looking for shortcuts. They bring "all of themselves" to what they do. Everything stops, and the moment is deeply satisfying.

"When I'm drawing I don't want to be anywhere else but right there doing that drawing," Gale said.

CAFE MILANO REGULARS

I used to think I was the only Cafe Milano regular, but when I began to really notice, I saw that there were several others at the early morning "shift."

Kathleen and Allan, a well-groomed couple in their forties, sit downstairs. They stand out, dressed for the business world in downtown San Francisco. It's obvious that they are a couple, but they don't talk to each other, each intent on the newspaper.

"What made you decide to come here?" I asked.

"Martin, the coffee, the ambiance, the newspaper, and the silence." Kathleen volunteered. "Friends laugh at our preoccupation with our coffee," she continued, "but this half hour ritual is terribly real—and important."

AN IMPERFECT, PERFECT PLACE

Today at Cafe Milano they're playing rap music and it's particularly loud, not at all the kind of music I like. And they've just painted the bathroom a bilious green with a darker blue-green railing. The effect is jarring. Is this management's latest attempt to ward off the attacks of graffiti?

In spite of all this, it's my "home away from home," and when I sit down surrounded by my piles of paper and look at the smiling face in the foam of my cappuccino, I am able to focus—perfectly happy in this imperfect place.

ART AS A TEACHER

LEARNING TO SEE

For as long as I can remember I've wanted to draw.

What I mean is I'd like to be able to make something look real. I have taken a lot of beginning drawing classes and I've had some wonderful teachers. However, by the end of each class almost every student can follow the instructions and draw realistically, and I am left frustrated. It's not that I'm devoid of artistic talent, but when I try to draw what I actually see in front of me, the work turns out cockeyed and lopsided.

"Sue, we've had this same conversation for years," says Joe, my drawing teacher. "You tell me you can't draw and I tell you that you draw fine. The particular way you see is *your* way. Trust it." His sincere assurance does me no good. I'm not satisfied. I believe there is some other way to draw that is better than my way. I *do* want to learn to draw realistically. I want to have a choice. And I'm willing to keep trying.

In December I decided to give myself a Christmas present, a mental health break from writing. Each day that month I would go in the studio and practice drawing a pear.

One pear.

I also wanted to experiment with color. My goal for the end of the month was to draw a pear that looked fat and delicious. My theory was that if I *limited my focus*, stared at that one pear, I would eventually be able to "see." I thought the key to "seeing" was to find the shadows, notice where the light and dark fell on the surface of the pear. And, if I could do that, a fat, rounded pear would emerge.

That didn't happen. I was having so much trouble seeing the actual shape of the pear that my husband took pity on me and drew an outline of a generic pear that I could trace.

At the end of the month I had forty-seven beautiful, richly colored pears painted in acrylic—a few nice enough, because of the luscious color, to give as Christmas presents, but all flat, except one, which I gave to my husband.

I had failed at my stated purpose, mastery of shape and shadow, but instead of frustration and a sense of time wasted, the month of struggle delivered many satisfactions.

Waking up each day knowing I was going to draw a pear changed the quality of my day. Total devotion to one task, even for a brief period of time—to stop the world—was enormously satisfying. I was carried along by clear *intention* and *genuine effort.*

Drawing the pear was a lot of effort—and I saw a value in that effort. When I wasn't laughing at myself for sitting in a dark room staring at a now rotting pear, I saw that perseverance and determination were strengths to be appreciated, whatever the outcome.

If I could practice "unattached intending"—not worrying about the *result*, staying focused exactly on what I was seeing—would a rounded pear appear?

When Richard first drew the outline of a pear for me, I had felt that was cheating. The pear wasn't really mine. But, somewhere in the course of that month, I accepted the fact that I wasn't able to learn everything at once.

Breaking an overwhelming task down into manageable steps was an immense help.

It's true I had failed at my larger ambition—to have the pear appear fat—but it no longer felt like a failure.

I was learning *small* things. And hopefully, with patience, I'd learn some more.

I thought again of Gale's one hundred luscious *round* pots and asked her to come to the studio. I described my battle to draw a pear. She listened. She then suggested I further limit my task. In order to see the shadows, I was to find a real pear whose shape I liked and paint the pear itself with white acrylic. Then I was to turn off the lights, all except one to highlight the pear, and, using a soft B lead pencil and paper strong enough to tolerate lots of erasing, try to see and draw the shadows.

The next week my "professor" returned and said I was still seeing too much—trying to get every nuance in, and, as a result, giving everything equal importance. "Still drowning in possibilities," she said.

"Squint!" she said the next week, after seeing how I was progressing. "See if you can focus on the larger masses."

"Linger!" was her next lesson. "Take your time. Keep going over the lines, move in the direction of the pear, feel the strokes as you're making them."

As the weeks went by she continued her instructions. "All through your experience of drawing the pear, you talk about the discomfort and struggle. Not once do you mention the experience of *loving* to draw. Loving the feeling of a pencil gliding on the paper, the sensual pleasure of it all!

"Yes, there is struggle, *tedium* in the process," she continued, "but there is also joy. And excitement in small discoveries along the way. Staying detached from the 'result' is easy when your process is as 'fat and delicious' as the pear itself." Her words made me sad.

I'm familiar with *struggle*.

"*Lingering* means intimacy," Gale continued. "It's having a relationship with each piece. You can't be parked in a 'red zone,' with your mind on the possibility of getting a parking ticket, at the same time you are drawing. It means losing a sense of time. It means starting a drawing at 9:00 A.M. and being so deeply engaged in it that you look up at your clock and see it's 2:30. Where did the time go? How come I'm not hungry? How come I didn't answer the phone?"

Most of us don't have the luxury of large chunks of time to do exactly what we want to do. The challenge is to find even ten minutes when the world stops, and for that moment, there is nothing else. How can we bring that quality to what time we have—making that limited time sacred?

Slowly, over time, sitting in my darkened studio, I began to see distinctions. After hundreds of minuscule adjustments, something resembling a pear did emerge. Someone looking at these pears might have thought, "Why all the fuss? My grandmother could do as well, if not better!" That's not the point. These ever-changing, imperfect pears are teaching me to appreciate the struggle, the willingness not to give up, to laugh at myself for the seriousness and determination with which I approach everything.

"Draw your pear, Sue, and work from your heart," Gale said.

The following Saturday I had a few unclaimed hours and decided to give myself an extra treat and work in the studio, copying a fresh and delicious looking pear made by the artist, Robert Kulicke. This was Kulicke's pear, not mine. I could relax. My job was to stare at the picture in front of me. For three hours nothing else mattered. I loved what I was doing. But even though his drawing was right in front of me, my pear was lopsided and looked like it wasn't resting on the table, and I soon became frustrated.

The next morning I went into the studio to make sure I'd cleaned everything up and was amazed to see my four Kulicke pears, looking alive, with their own spirit of ripe deliciousness.

I hadn't added anything—except time and distance.

Caught in the up-close struggle, I hadn't been able to step back and see what was there. Mine and not mine—it made no difference.

Several times on Sunday I went back to the studio to admire the pears.

MY WOBBLY BOWL

Sitting in a coffee house with Richard, I drew my generic rendering of a bowl. The bottom was round, not flat.

"Your bowl has no stability," Richard said. "It will move or even tip over the second you put something in it." He picked up his coffee cup and placed it in front of me on the table. "Your bowl doesn't have a solid base. A cup has a bottom that is flat."

He was right. Because my bowl's bottom is round, every time I put something in it the bowl changes. It's never the same. The bowl moves in relationship to everything else.

A MYSTERY SOLVED

All these years I had kept the experience of the white paintings close to my heart. I hadn't understood what they were trying to teach me, but when Richard said that about my wobbly bowl, a mystery that had eluded me for three years was suddenly clear.

After seeing the white paintings, I had gone out and bought every single catalogue of all Ryman's shows and read every word. I even wrote him a letter, and went to visit him in his studio in New York. "You don't have to know to feel it," Ryman had said. "You don't have to figure it out. You understand."

His work is not *about* anything else.

"It's the 'act of painting itself,'" that interests Ryman.

The paint, the material of the canvas, the brush, the brush strokes, the fasteners that will hold the picture in place, how the picture is placed on the wall, the relationship of each picture to the other—the light, how the picture will change at different times of the day—the "all of it."

"Everything affects everything else."

Everything counts.

When Gale and I went to see a major retrospective of Ryman's work at the San Francisco Museum of Modern Art, Gale stood in front of one of my favorite paintings, one that is particularly white, and for ten minutes I listened as she described all the nuance and color that was present in the white.

Standing there I again felt the "immensity within ourselves" that I had read about and hadn't understood. But at that moment, I was aware of something essential, some deep connection we all share.

Everything counts.

Everyone counts.

GENEROSITY

Since my first meeting with Yvonne, who mentioned that "generosity was the ground for everything," I've been thinking about generosity in a new way.

Last month my husband Richard and I decided at age sixty and sixty-three, it was finally time to be grown up and responsible. Neither of us are practical about business or financial matters. We went to a lawyer and started the process of making a will and a living trust for our sons.

"What would you like to do in case there's an 'exploding turkey?'" the lawyer asked.

"Exploding turkey?" I asked.

"*What if* the whole family was together at Thanksgiving and the turkey exploded?" he asked. "If the four of you were killed at that moment, who would you want to have your worldly goods?"

That turned out to be a terrific assignment. A chance to think about the people in our lives, a chance to be grateful and express our gratitude.

I decided to create a new ritual. I would stop at the end of the day, even a particularly difficult day, and make a list: a gratitude list. Who or what do I have to be grateful for today?

My son Michael told me about his girlfriend's father, a wanderer, who had left the family and had never really had a home of his own. She hadn't seen very much of him in her life. He's sixty-seven years old and earns his living transporting trucks and cars across America. Recently he came to pay her a visit.

"Harriet's father fills the trucks with flowering bulbs," Michael told me.

Immediately my mind made up a story about an enterprising person selling bulbs along his route. But Harriet's father plants these bulbs along the way, anonymously, as he crisscrosses America—a Johnny Appleseed of the highways.

"Can you tell me more about him?" I asked Harriet.

"He was inaccessible and distant when I was young, wasn't really there for me," she told me when we met. "He thinks a lot about doing things for me and means to get in touch, but he never gets around to it. What pleases me is that this time he followed through. He expressed something of his own. Planting bulbs is *his*—not something someone asked or forced him to do."

Then she added, "I didn't see the beauty of his planting the bulbs, the giving part of it, till I casually mentioned it to Michael and he told you, and you wanted to write about it. You're making me notice. I just took it for granted.

"That's the kind of thing he would do. He does have a soft side," she said wistfully. "Your noticing helps make his softer side apparent. He never killed anything. He'd take a house fly outside in the summer, where there were many flies, and take a snake he found in the basement and bring it outside and wish it well.

"I wonder how many other things he's done that I haven't noticed!"

Now, when Harriet sees daffodils and crocuses growing along a freeway she thinks of him and smiles.

"Sometimes you need someone else's eyes to show you the beauty that's been in front of you all the time," she added.

Maybe the most sacred things are the hardest to see, because they are so obvious.

My son David sends a card almost every week to his grandmother, aged eighty-nine. I don't know how this ritual got started, but I do know he spends a lot of time looking for just the right card, one he thinks will please her. This *practice* has been going on for more than three years, and he says it's a challenge to keep finding "special" new cards.

This year on her birthday David went east to visit his grandmother. "I never understood how much getting a card means to Grandma," he told us when he returned. "She looks forward to checking the mail. I could really see how happy she was when she got a few birthday cards."

I was tempted to leave this story out. Sending a card to your grandmother? But that's just the point. We all have our own version of David's card to his grandmother. Too often we take these small acts of kindness for granted. We think we have to have a large achievement or gift to offer others.

Small kindnesses make a difference—they have echoes out of proportion to the effort they take.

"We do not great things, we do only small things with great love," Mother Teresa said.

Several years ago I made a white, cotton-stuffed container, complete with big droopy handles, and decided it would be used as an irreverent, unexpected flowerpot. It has become a beloved object—part of my family—and sits on a glass table in the living room. By now the batting is peeping out where too many Clorox soakings have eaten away at the cotton material.

A *ritual* has developed around the pot.

Once a week, before I clean the house, I go to a small florist to buy one batch of white daisies. The flowers cost between $1.50 and $2.00 depending on the season; the young woman treats this order with the same respect and loving attention as she would if she were making a mix of the most exotic flowers. I love watching her move slowly and deliberately, adding baby's breath to the mix, carefully intertwining each stalk so the tiny dots of white mixed with the daisy with the yellow center become a work of art—an offering that looks beautiful and feels abundant.

Each time I thank her for her generosity. I return home happy—ready to clean my house. "Where is the young lady?" I ask, disappointed, as I come into the store, looking for my friend. "She's out on her lunch break," I am told. Another woman puts the order together. When I mention adding baby's breath she takes a batch and brusquely sticks them in next to the bunch of daisies.

The same few flowers and the same few additions, but such a different result.

MITZI'S GIFT

My friendship with Mitzi didn't just happen. We didn't "connect" at first. We didn't find each other the least bit interesting.

But we met again, unexpectedly, at a friend's cooking class. Neither of us were cooks and probably really didn't care that much about cooking, but we went anyway, willing to give it a try. We had a lot of fun together being slightly rebellious in that class. We discovered we were fellow spirits.

Neither of us became great cooks, but we became good friends.

Mitzi *is* generosity.

I've heard of people who have "guides," but these guides are usually invisible, or healers or shamans. My special guide is quite visible and the form she takes is a small (under five feet tall) roundish seventy-three-year-old woman. With sparkling eyes, a mind that is quick, and thoughts that are deep—she is clear as a bell, one of those sounds that I remember hearing in a Zen temple that has ripples of aftereffects.

Wise words pour out of her as naturally as doubts pour out of me. Each week I bring a problem or a scattered thought and she listens.

Mitzi really *listens*.

As a result, I have the experience of being *heard* by another person—a huge gift.

GENEROSITY

I gave a talk to a book club in Oakland. All the members had lost their homes, lost everything in the terrible Oakland-Berkeley Hills fire of 1991. They lost pictures, momentos, diplomas, records—all the little and big things that made up their history and the history of their parents and grandparents.

One of the club members described having given a precious object as a gift to a friend. She had treasured the porcelain piece and almost didn't give it away because she loved it so much. After the fire her friend returned the object. Another woman told the group she gave away the things she didn't like and, after the fire, these same things were returned to her.

A WOMAN WITHOUT A HOME

There's another early morning "regular" at Cafe Milano. I see her almost every day and I wanted to talk with her, but sensed she was private. She always looks neat, but I often wondered if she was a person without a home. She sits upstairs, at the opposite side of the room from me, either looking intently outside at the view or engrossed in her readings and writing.

One Saturday morning I decided this would be the day to walk over and ask if we could talk for a few moments about the role of Cafe Milano in her life. By chance she walked across the room and asked if I had a pen she could borrow. "I see we both come here almost every day," I began. "I've been meaning to ask you why you chose Cafe Milano?"

"I love the light," she said. "It's easier to concentrate when the light comes in. It's uplifting. I also love looking out the window. Looking outside I have a bird's-eye view of life, and I sit here planning my day.

"The light lifts you off everyday life," she continued.

"I come for focus. I try to have something to do. I'm committed to studying something every day." She told me a little bit about her life before, when she was a dental hygienist, "one of those really happy times. When I had a life with possibilities."

I learned she lives in a shelter. She has to leave by 7:00 A.M. "Ready to meet the world." She likes Cafe Milano because she's treated like an individual here. "People are pleasant to me.

It proves you exist. Sometimes when I have no money they give me a coffee."

Then she quickly adds, "You'd better not say that. I don't want anyone to get in trouble. In the back of my mind I think it's a little bit like a loan."

"I dream of the day when my life is straightened out and I can walk in here and say 'This is what I owe you,' put $500 in the tip jar, and say 'THANK YOU.'"

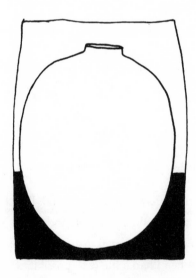

ACCEPTANCE

One week after the terrible Oakland-Berkeley Hills fire, I met Helen, a woman my age, on the street in Berkeley. She walked up to me and said, "I heard you talk at the Women's National Book Association last month. We lost our home in the fire. We lost everything." She took a breath and continued, "I loved *Plain and Simple*. I kept it next to my bed and I'm going to reread it when my life is normal again."

I stood there listening, not knowing what to say. The fire had left our community in shock. You could tell by the look in a person's eyes who had lost everything. But the look in Helen's eyes was different.

"There aren't many people I can say this to," she continued, "I certainly can't say it to my husband, who is devastated by the fire, but I think I can say it to you." She took a long, deep breath. "I have to trust that something good will come out of this," she said, and then repeated, "I think something good will come out of this."

Helen didn't say she wasn't grieving. Everything—every family photograph, quilt, a grandfather clock designed and built by her husband, all the hand-knit sweaters that had kept her warm—all were gone.

"The fire forced me to look at *what really matters*," Helen said.

Later, when I heard she had moved into her new home, I sent Helen a copy of *Plain and Simple*. A few times a year we meet by chance in the street and stop to say hello. "Ever since we first met," I told her last week, "I always begin my talks with your words about how the fire *forced* you to look at what really matters. Just as going to live with the Amish had forced me, ever so much more gently, to question all my assumptions about what goes into a good life.

"I have to tell you, a great deal of good *has* come out of the fire," she said.

I asked her to come to my house and tell me more about what has happened since the fire.

She accepted my invitation and we talked for two hours. I mostly listened.

A RADICAL CONCEPT

When I set out on this journey I was an *active* seeker. To be active, to *do*, was ingrained in me. I trusted I would find teachers, but not without my working hard *all* the time.

When a friend said, "Being doesn't exact a price," I hardly understood what she was saying.

The day after I met Helen, a statement by the monk Thomas Merton stared out at me from a book I was reading. An essential principle of the begging bowl, he said, is that a monk *accepts*, with gratitude, whatever is given.

This seemed a radical concept.

No matter what you are given—things no one would want in their bowl—you learn to accept—and feel grateful. Could I accept the idea that good things could come out of a catastrophe?

LOST THINGS KEEP APPEARING

"After the fire one of the things that pleased me so much," Helen said, "was that all my favorite recipes came back to me. Just three days ago I went to a lecture with a friend and she said, 'Oh, I was thinking about you last night because I made your lemon ice cream.'

" 'Oh, you have that recipe?' I thought it was gone forever. Another recipe that came back was for my mother-in-law's cannelloni, which she gave me long before I married my husband.

"I was a pattern-drafting teacher in an adult education pro-gram, and I just retired in July, and the same thing happened with patterns. When I was teaching, if I saw something stylish, a wonderful coat, for example, I would borrow it from a friend, draft a pattern, demonstrate it to the class and several people would make their own pattern. Right after the fire many students called to ask, 'What patterns do you want?'

"The pleasure of sharing comes from wanting to share. But it certainly gave me tremendous delight to have some of these lost things come back."

"Good deeds have echoes," my husband said, when I told him about Helen and her students.

WHY WASTE TIME BEING UNHAPPY?

Helen told me about one of her neighbors who had also lost her home and now spent a lot of time complaining. "After the fire," Helen told her friend, "I don't think we have time to waste being unhappy about decisions we've made."

What a wonderful sentence. If I was the kind of person who pastes important sayings on her refrigerator door, that's what I'd place there: *I don't think we have time to waste being unhappy.*

I thought of Yvonne's questions.

Why be unhappy about something you can change?

Why be unhappy about something you can't change?

123

"It's a contstant process of asking myself *what is important,*" Helen continued. "I didn't have to do that before. It was as if I was on a moving escalator at the L.A. airport, always racing through my life, having fun, but not really stopping to savor or distill what was important. It's all out there, everything I need, but I didn't see it because I was going too fast."

As I listened, I kept hearing her question, *"Why waste time being unhappy?"*

"I think that's one of the gifts of this fire experience," she added. "It fine tunes my attitude about the remainder of my life."

CHILD'S SKULL BOWL

I saw a bowl from Tibet made from a child's skull. It had beautifully carved silver inlay around the outer rim and a turquoise stone placed in the center. The bowl is thought to have the capacity to hear anything, however sad, however horrible.

Followers of Tibetan Buddhism believe that anything placed in these ritual objects can be healed and transformed into compassionate understanding.

"What I am learning is not 'light-bulb joy,'" Helen said that same day. "Nothing really dramatic, but the experiences add up to the beginning of wisdom." She thought again about the day of the fire. "If I use the word 'searching,' someone might think I'm not content. My searching is more like that of a monk. I'm not driven in the search, but hope to keep learning things along the way."

"After my visits to the Amish," I told her, "I had expected to be transformed. I expected to see *big* changes. Instead, I found little changes, and a new appreciation of all the things I had taken for granted."

Helen smiled. "Maybe that's the beginning of wisdom. There are no answers, there are just experiences."

CULTIVATE YOUR GARDEN

An announcement came today for an art show that included Gale's work—drawings of apples, eggplant, eggs, garlic, oranges, and squash.

CULTIVATE YOUR GARDEN

The word *cultivate* jumped off the card.

I thought of Helen and her long view in the midst of dreadful circumstances, how she *cultivated* gratitude.

Could I cultivate and nurture within myself the attitude of a monk who carries a begging bowl? Could I cultivate a way of accepting whatever is placed in my bowl so that I could learn from anything?

Could I put aside, for a while, my natural inclination to work hard all the time?

Could I just *be* with the bowl.

Could I be open to receive?

A P.S. FROM HELEN

The day I was to hand in this manuscript Helen called. "The fire solved a lot of problems," she said. "That may sound strange, but the fire forced us to do things that would have been difficult to do in the future. My husband and I came out stronger, united—a team." She continued. "I'm immensely grateful for every detail in our lives that gives us pleasure.

"This is probably the happiest time in our life."

SMALL MIRACLES

"Maybe I wrote *Everyday Sacred* to learn more about miracles," I said in the prologue.

I wanted a *big* miracle, one that would last, but one of the characteristics of a big miracle, the kind I had hoped for, is "its sudden appearance and disappearance within the natural order." Instead, to my surprise, I began to discover the power of *small* things.

A friend made a pilgrimage to India. She saw many holy places, but her favorite was a mound made up of little pebbles, not one of them beautiful or exotic. For hundreds of years pilgrims had come to this site and each placed a tiny stone offering on the mound. The accumulation of these little stones became a "sacred" place.

I saw those little stones as stepping stones.

Stepping stones toward a new way of *seeing*.

Small changes in behavior, attitude, feelings, can, like the little pebbles, add up to another kind of miracle. Small miracles do build up and they can last.

When I stopped waiting for something "significant" to happen, and instead began noticing what *was* happening, not what I wished was happening, a series of small miracles occurred.

When I began to trust what I was doing even when it didn't seem to make sense, when I understood that what I was doing was seeking, then what I was seeking was shown to me.

People knocked on my door and said, "Would you like this?" Chance occurrences, unexpected meetings made me feel I was not alone.

When I trusted I was doing something of value, goals and timetables had a way of taking care of themselves.

Jung called them "meaningful coincidences." Peter, a Swiss friend, described the German word *zufall,* which roughly translates as "to fall into." "Something falls to you," he said, "not as something you caused, but a coincidence you are ready to accept and absorb in your life." I realized he was describing serendipity. I notice these moments come when I'm not demanding or insistent that they come.

Today, stapled on a telephone pole crowded with other posters, I saw:

"Allow—for the possibilities."

SWEAT LODGE

I am a "fear type" who doesn't look afraid.

In the past, my strategy has been to avoid fear or other strong feelings that make me uncomfortable, using whatever strategy I can think of. Usually I just try to keep busy.

I was about to leave Berkeley for a month, when a friend asked if I wanted to come to a sweat lodge that Saturday. The timing wasn't good and I didn't know much about the ceremony, but I had a romantic image of heat, American Indian wisdom, wholeness—and a chance to bless my journey.

My friend, who had participated in the sweat lodge ceremony many times, assured me the people were sympathetic. The rural Sonoma county setting had the spare vastness of a New Mexico landscape. The ceremony would be conducted by a Lakota Sioux woman.

One at a time, the twelve of us crouched to get through a small flap in the canvas door and entered a tepee-like structure. Where I sat cross-legged on the earthen floor, my head practically touched the ceiling of the tent. The twelve of us formed a circle around a large fire pit. Very slowly a woman began carrying in lava rocks on something that looked like an elongated pizza carrier, placing each one of them carefully in the center of the fire pit.

While she was doing this there was a bit of chanting and a few instructions, and then the leader told us that if we chose to

130

leave at any point in the ceremony, we would not be allowed to return.

Feeling rather pleased with myself that at sixty I was willing, even eager, to take on an unexpected adventure, something quite foreign to anything I had ever done, I sat there, calm, anticipating an interesting "event." When the last of the twenty-eight coals was placed in the pit, the woman left, closing the flap of the door behind her.

Total darkness.

Water poured on the rocks created a whoosh of furious steam heat. Heat permeating every air space. I love steam baths, so I had looked forward to this part of the ritual. It took only four minutes for me to be afraid.

Very afraid.

My friend had suggested that if it got too hot, I could lie down on the earthen floor. I tried that but it made no difference. I tried poking my fingers under a tiny opening at the bottom of the tent, hoping that would relieve my growing anxiety, but nothing worked.

This fear wasn't attached to any thoughts except *how* I was going to survive.

The last thought I had was that *if* I managed to get out I wouldn't be hard on myself. I had done the best I could. Then, no thoughts. Only fear. Raw, palpable, free-floating fear in every cell—and darkness.

Too paralyzed, or too civilized, to yell "let me out," I was half aware of people talking with great feeling, telling what had brought them here. Each asked for guidance and a blessing from the leader, and the power she represented.

My own civilized notion of why I was here was gone. I had thought it was to ask a blessing for my journey and for the book I was writing, but now, lying on the ground, my heart pounding so hard I thought it might explode, I didn't think I was even in a condition to speak. My friend, sitting next to me, spoke, in a firm voice I had never heard her use before.

When it was my turn I heard myself, in a quiet, slow, tiny, soft, voice say,

"*I am very afraid.* I'm not sure I can stay. I am very, very frightened."

"Come and sit next to me," said the leader, who was sitting next to the exit door. She spoke some wise words, none of which I can remember now, as I crawled halfway around the circle to where she was, feeling at the time it was the most natural of things to be doing. I lay down very still, still needing the security of the cooler ground for support.

Someone put a steady hand on my leg—and that hand stayed there, not moving, for the rest of the ritual. In the darkness I never saw who that person was. That steady hand, of a man or a woman, I never learned who it was, was a great help.

Time passed.

The enormity of the fear began to diminish.

More chanting, a long wooden pipe handed from person to person, prayers, and the ceremony was over. The fear began to be bearable. I stepped outside and the night air was cool and welcoming.

I felt calm.

Having no place to hide, I had felt my fear and the "fear cracked open."

A giant weight had lifted off my shoulders. A huge chunk of fear I had carried just below the surface for a long time had been dislodged. Whether this fear had anything to do with my harsh judge, I didn't know, but suddenly I felt like I was traveling though life with a lighter knapsack.

Recently I read a description of a sweat lodge: "You will probably die during the ceremony," the Indian leader had said. "And today is, after all, a good day to die." That did not sound overly dramatic to me. If anyone had warned me about what might happen during the sweat lodge ceremony, I wouldn't have taken the risk.

I saw a curious relationship; the more I was able to stay with, not move away from, uncomfortable feelings, the more I was also able to feel happy and alive.

Remembering how calm I felt when I stepped out into the night air after being in the sweat lodge, I now know I don't have to wait for an exotic ceremony to turn toward, rather than away from, difficult feelings.

I have a chance almost any day.

DOORS OPEN INWARD

Why is it sometimes harder to accept our strengths than our weaknesses?

"Doors open inward," Ekai told me a long time ago, and then he added, "Sue, you cannot find what is not already there."

At the time I felt empty, unable to admit that I did have a strong, innate, and informed sense of what I needed to find. It was hard to accept that I knew more than I thought I knew.

We all know more than we think we know.

When I thought I had lost Ekai's rakusu, I panicked. "You have to take the qualities you saw in Ekai's gift, the qualities you think are outside yourself, and bring them inside," a voice inside me had said.

The Moroccan bowl, Gale's pot, Ekai's rakusu, the smiling face in the cappuccino, the white paintings—were outward symbols of qualities I had been looking for inside. They gave form to what was there inside, waiting to be uncovered.

Mitzi described a *Self Assessment* workshop she gave. She asked the participants to list their achievements—the things they felt good about. "Most people omitted things that came easily and naturally to them," she said, "They see an achievement only when there were difficulties."

Perhaps our natural gifts elude us because they *are* so obvious.

NANCY'S DOOR STORY

When I work, I hardly ever take a proper break for lunch. To celebrate handing the manuscript over to my agent, I said "yes" when a friend invited me to lunch. Two other women came that I didn't know, and we spent a few hours together, unexpectedly telling each other stories that have moved us.

That morning I had been working on *Doors Open Inward*. As I told them about this journey—learning to trust things that outwardly didn't seem to make sense—I instinctively placed my hands together, forming a bowl with my hands, telling them of the importance of the begging bowl in my life. One of the guests understood the gesture and placed this story in my bowl.

It was mid-December, and her best friend had just died of pancreatic cancer. At the time she was working as the assistant head of a Montessori school in Connecticut. "When I went to work that week, I did something I had never done before. I closed the door to my office. My fellow teachers understood. No one attempted to disturb me.

"My office looked out over the front of the school with high, floor-to-ceiling windows, and I would sit at my desk and watch each morning as the yellow school bus pulled in front and its cargo of small children tumbled out carrying their Care Bear lunch boxes, mittens dangling from strings, and backpacks sporting super heroes. While mothers laughed and plotted their days together, some of the children made the ritual stop to swing on the low-slung dogwood tree branch before entering the building.

"As the week progressed I found myself getting angrier and angrier:

"*Didn't they understand?*

"The world was not the same; something had changed. *Why didn't they see?*

"On Friday morning there was a small tap on my door. I could tell by the sound and the placement that it was a small child. I really didn't want to open the door, but I took a deep breath and gritted my teeth, and when I opened the door there was three-year-old Caroline, with a plate of Christmas cookies in her hand. 'Hello Nancy, I just wanted to give you these Christmas cookies.'

"As I bent down to receive the cookies, Caroline whispered in my ear, 'And I just wanted to ask you how come your door's closed?'

"I looked at Caroline and said. 'I don't know why it's closed, Caroline. Let's open it.'

"That three-year-old child gave me a gift that I will have with me forever. Alone, I never could have opened that door. Yet the lesson I took into my heart will continue to serve me.

"There is a world out there worth living.

"Although I may need to retreat from time to time, I will always keep the door ajar, never completely closed."

A spirit of generosity filled the room that afternoon as we sat around telling each other our stories, encouraging stories. Maybe *Everyday Sacred* is also about finding friends, making friends our teachers.

Visiting another friend, Betsy, I found myself making a begging bowl gesture with my hands and talking to her about the image of the begging bowl and learning to accept whatever comes into my bowl. She said the gesture reminded her of an old children's tale called Stone Soup. The tale goes like this:

> Before the stranger came, everyone in the small village was hungry.
>
> No one had enough to eat; each person hoarded what little he had. And the peasants feared strangers. A man who was an outsider came to stay in the village. One day he began boiling water in a very large pot. He then proceeded slowly and carefully to add very large stones, one at a time. One of the villagers came by to look and stood for a very long time, watching him stir the mixture. Finally the villager asked, "What are you doing?" "I'm making stone soup," was the stranger's reply. "It's still missing something, but would you like to try some?" The villager tasted the soup and agreed. Something was still missing.
>
> "Maybe I could go home and bring you a few carrots to add to the soup," the man offered.
>
> One by one the other villagers came. Each observed what the stranger was doing, and each asked about the odd soup made with very large stones. After a while each of the villagers offered to bring a little of what they could spare to add to the soup. One brought a few potatoes, another an

onion, a cabbage, on and on until there were many rich and varied ingredients in the soup.

As they waited for the soup to be ready, the villagers gathered together around the pot, telling each other stories, feeling they were all a part of a celebration. Indeed, the soup was tasty and there was enough for all. They were nourished by the delicious meal and the teamwork that had made it possible.

"We shall never go hungry again now that we know how to make soup from stones."

Maybe what I have been doing for the last three years is making stone soup.

I have walked around telling everyone I met a story.

"Images came before the words," the story began. A blinking light, EVERYDAY SACRED, and then the image of a begging bowl reached out and grabbed my heart. I told everyone that I felt like a monk, setting out early each morning with my begging bowl in my hands.

I was still searching for something and still not sure what I was searching for. People listened to my story. They had the wonderful capacity to suspend judgment. Maybe I supplied the stones for the soup. I know I listened for stories that might fill my bowl.

Friends, with great generosity, offered their carrots and cabbage and onions and potatoes. When everyone gave something, the *whole* was richer than the individual ingredients.

Together we made a good soup.

I love the story of *Stone Soup* because it is filled with wonder. There will always be magic stones if we just look around and see them. The *wonder* is that these stones are all around us.

Why put a limit on believing?

If you *believe,* you begin to look. And you begin to *see* what has been there all the time.

KEVIN'S CRACKED POTS

My friend Loie has a beautiful black bowl, a large cauldron, hand-burnished with a patina that takes a great deal of time and attention to achieve. American Indians do this kind of burnishing. They work on their bowls by hand-polishing and rubbing them for a very long time until a glass-like shine appears. The pot's depth and glow seems to come from within.

Loie's black bowl makes me think of an ancient soul.

Each time I visit Loie I stop and say hello to this pot. When I look closely, I can see it has been cracked and glued back together. "That's my friend Kevin's pot," Loie told me on one visit. "Kevin makes cracked pots."

"Do you think I could visit him?" I ask, excited.

We went to see Kevin together; he had an open broad face that exuded light. He talked about how horrified he had been when the bowl he was making for Loie cracked. "This can't be. This can't crack!" he repeated, reenacting the scene of destruction. "After all the labor and love that went into it."

This had been happening a lot. Usually Kevin would start again, making a brand new pot, but when the bowl he made for

Loie cracked, he asked whether she would mind if the bowl was broken and mended again.

Loie had traveled the world and remembered her visit to the mountains of Pakistan. She saw cracked teapots that had been mended. The cracks were filled with metal and they became watertight. These mended teapots were revered treasures. "Oh, yes," she answered, "that's a great idea."

This was the permission Kevin needed.

Before, he had resisted doing anything with his broken pots because a potter he really respected was making wonderfully colored, cracked pots that he glued back together, and Kevin didn't want to copy his style. "In the ceramic world we want to be original. We want to discover some new technique—something all our own." It took Kevin a long time to realize it was okay for him to mend his pots.

"I had to melt into allowing myself to accept what was happening, instead of my ego saying 'I have to find something new.' I wanted to make certain that I was following my own path.

"As I grew and developed, I realized I couldn't do anyone's pots but my own. Now I love cracking them. It suits a part of my personality, my destructive side."

"How does your destructive side find its way into your work?" I asked, very curious.

"Before I acted out unconsciously. And it wasn't good for me. I had a really strong desire to make pots. But I would sabotage myself by taking unnecessary risks, and I'd have lots of accidents. I would drop nearly completed pots, I would blow them up by raising the kiln too fast, and I simply wouldn't finish some pots. I didn't understand what was happening.

"I didn't get rid of my destructive side. I just use it more constructively."

"How do you actually crack them?" I asked.

"I work on the wheel for a long time to get grace and beauty in the form. Once the pots are fired in the kiln, I lay a towel on the cement floor of my studio, and then I take the pot in both hands and bang the pot until it cracks.

"Once I hear the crack I get very nervous. I've intentionally destroyed what I've made. I know that it's not whole anymore. There's no going back. I continue banging until the pot falls into many pieces. I fire these pieces in a rake kiln or in sawdust. Then I glue the little pieces together and still have a form that makes sense when it's done.

"I surrender to the saboteur.

"I surrender to the destructive side, not knowing how the pot's going to come out. That side of me, the part that is very hard on myself, needed to be embraced. And I've had to love that part of myself, or at least acknowledge and accept it.

"Cracking of the pots gave that saboteur a voice.

"I was gluing one of the cracked pots today and I dropped it.

143

'Oh, I dropped it,' I said to myself. I didn't beat myself up, and I didn't say I was an awful person. I just said, 'Oh, I dropped it. The saboteur's here!'"

Once Kevin gave himself permission, he noticed he wasn't ruining so many pieces.

Then he added, with much feeling, "I think it's more than that. It's trusting that it's going to work. Before, I would work and work and think I was on the right track, and then in the morning I'd think 'How did the pots get so awful overnight?' Now something has shifted. I can say 'I made this pot. And it's wonderful.'

"As soon as I was less critical of myself," Kevin continued, "I viewed the pots with different eyes. They're me!"

The pots became a tool for healing.

"They're like a barometer for me now. It's one thing to constructively critique myself, but another to be harshly critical of the work. Now I know that if I make a pot and I see it as beautiful or wonderful, and then the next day I don't feel that it's wonderful, it means that there is some part of me that I'm not loving.

The pot is just a reflection of me."

145

ANDREA

Andrea, a friend of Kevin's, teaches painting to a group of young kids from troubled backgrounds. She remembers one student, a thirteen-year-old boy, who made glorious paintings and then destroyed them.

"I hate it and it's ugly," he would shout, as he ripped everything up.

Andrea got smarter; when she saw the child was about to finish a painting she took it away from him, saying: "You're not allowed to destroy this painting until the two of us have a chance to talk about it." She made a waiting rule: "I will keep this for you, for now, because right now you don't know how precious it is."

The boy would scream at her, "You're a liar!"

"It is beautiful," Andrea would answer in a calm and reassuring voice. "I know more about art than you, because I have more experience."

Pretty soon the child wasn't ripping his paintings up. She could see the change in his eyes. He had begun to realize that someone cared about him. So he started to care—just a tiny bit.

"The little step of love," Kevin elaborated, "one tiny little step. We can not imagine how important and precious it is to care about each other." I showed Kevin a quote I had just written down from Van Gogh to his brother.

"I tell you the more I think, the more I feel that there is nothing more truly artistic than to love people."

A GIFT IN MOTION

I felt so much gratitude to Kevin for his offering, but felt the exchange was uneven—I had done nothing for him. When we next met he told me: "It's been a wonderful thing for me, talking to you. Something about your coming and asking me all those questions brought all the work I've been doing in the studio, and in my personal and spirit life, home again. You helped me to see how much cracking pots served to melt my heart."

A gift was in motion.

In my wallet, on the front of the computer, and in my notebook I carry around a fragment of a quote:

"What you bring to something—not what you get from it."

The begging bowl was teaching me a new kind of generosity. I was learning that what we *bring* to our work, friendships, our family, will directly affect what we get from these relationships.

Today, in the mail, just before Christmas, came a card from my publisher. As I opened the envelope, eager to read what was printed, out fell a wondrous number of many sized, small paper gold stars.

"That which we withhold is withheld from us; that which we give is given back to us a thousandfold."

My mother taught me that it was a strength to be independent, to *not* ask for help. I had even been uncomfortable receiving a gift, dreading having to open it in front of others. I am learning that if we ask for help, we can help others. Accepting other people's generosity is a form of generosity.

How we receive a gift can be a gift to the giver.

THE BOWLS OF PURI

Another friend, also named Betsey, told me about the small town of Puri in India, which has a very important temple that is visited by many pilgrims every day. The potters in Puri make bowls for the pilgrims to eat out of, and the bowls are broken after they are used. This is because once they are used to feed the pilgrims, the bowls become holy and can't be used for ordinary meals.

The potters' life work is making bowls not to be broken, but to be holy.

I don't always listen when a voice says "pay attention." When I do, I find myself led in unexpected directions. I am not a student of tea, or an expert on Zen tea bowls, and I don't meditate. But something about the spartan simplicity of the tea house, the ceremony done with loving attention to details, and the handsome tea bowls captures my imagination.

I was intrigued reading about the early Japanese Zen masters who went to Korea. How were they able to have "fresh eyes," to look at hundreds and hundreds of "ordinary" Korean rice bowls and *see* the ones that had particular beauty? These clay bowls were made by potters, humble craftsmen following a tradition centuries old, who made the same form two hundred times a day, quickly and with many imperfections.

These potters did not sign their work. Their job was to make hardy bowls that would be useful and last. Samurai warriors, offered a choice between vast land holdings or some of these early Korean tea bowls, often chose the bowls. These bowls are now revered treasures in Japan.

The early Zen masters could see the beauty emanating from inside the bowl. They appreciated these cracked, bumpy, uneven pots. They could see irregularity as a gift—an empty space, a place for mystery.

EVERY DAY

I always knew the image for the cover of this book would be a bowl. But what bowl? One of Gale's one hundred pots, a cracked pot of Kevin's, one of my own small Raku begging bowls—or even one of those handsome Japanese tea bowls I admire. I wrote to Christy, a teacher of the tea ceremony. She called and said that she knew of the perfect bowl.

"It is very plain yet strong, made by the abbot of Myokian, the temple where Rikyu's tearoom remains. The abbot gave it the name *Yokihi.*

"*Yokihi* literally means 'a good day.'

"It comes from the phrase 'every day is a good day.' "

She paused for a moment and then added, "We ourselves make each day what it is. The fortunate and unfortunate will always be with us, but our responses—maintaining dignity and equilibrium—to whatever befalls us, determine whether the day is good or not."

RAKU

Three weeks before this book was to be finished, a bright pink flyer arrived in the mail, announcing that Kevin and his friend and fellow artist, Nancy, were giving a workshop in Raku.

I was busy working on last minute changes in the manuscript, but I signed up. If Kevin had called the class "How to make chicken soup" I would have signed up. Kevin knew something and I wanted to learn more about it.

Firing a Raku kiln is a lesson in uncertainty.

Your pots may explode because you must open the kiln at its hottest temperature, actually seeing the pot on fire. You retrieve it directly from the glowing heat, being careful not to drop the molten object, and plunge it into a metal garbage can stuffed with torn newspapers. The mixture ignites immediately.

There's a randomness which sometimes produces glorious results.

"The fire seals the fate of the pot," Kevin said.

We fired many kilns that day. Easily, without thinking, without effort, I made twenty small begging bowls. When it was time for the last firing, Kevin and Nancy asked if we wanted to add toxic chemicals to the fire. They might create dramatic effects.

My immediate response was, "Of course not."

Then I remembered the "esoteric bowl" practice—symbolically gathering our very worst and best qualities, and then, with a huge knife—a "knife of wisdom"—chopping and chopping until the whole turns into ambrosia.

"Yes," I said, "let's add the *terrible* to the mix."

We took turns lifting our pieces out of the fire. As I stared into the kiln, I was surprised to hear myself say, silently, in florid prose, "Let the fire burn away any pretense. Let the fire burn away any concern about what they will think. Instead, stand exactly as I am, full of impurities, tender as a new day."

Out of that last kiln came lumpy, bumpy, pockmarked, and luminous little begging bowls, quite unlike the smooth white ceramics I had always made. Each startlingly, singularly different, a mass of unexpected color, rich and vibrant.

These perfectly imperfect little begging bowls, with all their impurities, were bursting with life. They were symbols of a soul search—toward acceptance. A celebration indeed, in the best sense, of our humanness.

"You don't know ahead of time how cracking a pot can affect your life," Kevin had said, the first time we met.

Now, in the middle of the Raku class, he asked, "Is anyone interested in cracking pots?"

We would do the cracking the following week, using unglazed pots we'd either made that day or brought from home. I looked in my studio; it was hard to choose a good pot, knowing it would be broken.

I found four fairly large bowls, complete with cobwebs, abandoned, caught in the shift from my studio work to writing. The next Sunday, when the time came to crack my first bowl, Kevin placed a small, thin, very used white towel on the cement floor, first shooing his dog, Maggie, off the towel. I was to hold my bowl firmly in two hands and then bang the bowl on the floor.

I held my breath.

Though I acted "as if" my intention was to really crack the pot, I could feel my body constrict. I could feel myself holding back. "You'll have to bang harder," Kevin said.

"LET GO!" I shouted to myself silently.

"After all it's only a piece of clay. It wouldn't be tragic if it did shatter." I tried a second time. Again, no success. "You're hanging on so tenaciously," my judging mind said, "as if your life depended on keeping the bowl just the way it is."

I say I want to change, and then, when I'm unexpectedly given the opportunity to try new behavior, I hold on to an old, familiar way as if my life depended on it.

"Keep banging till it cracks," Kevin said, and I could feel encouragement in his voice.

On the fifth attempt the bowl cracked.

The effect of the bowl cracking was visceral. I took a long deep breath, feeling great relief—a release. Release from what? I didn't know, but the expression "*fear cracked open*" came to mind. Perhaps my judge was loosening her grip on me.

Now I had two pieces. "Should I do more?" I asked.

"Yes."

There was no resistance the next time. A barrier had come down. With ease and just the right amount of force the next pieces broke easily. Nine pieces. I knew that was enough.

"*Save the slivers*," Kevin said. "These little pieces are important."

"Why bother saving them, they're so small?" I asked, as I watched Kevin carefully collect the slivers and put them into an envelope for safekeeping. "If the piece is there, we'll have a use for it. When we're putting the bowl together it is necessary to have all the parts."

Next, I carefully placed the nine large broken pieces in a low, round metal bucket filled with wood chips and lit a match. Kevin set the chips on fire. The fire danced and touched and affected each piece differently depending on which parts were closest to the flame. I used long tongs and asbestos gloves to pick up the pieces when they looked burned enough, and then placed them on the ground until they cooled off.

As we were about to glue the first two pieces together, Kevin showed me how to mix equal parts of two epoxies that shipbuilders use. They would hold "forever." Then I was to spread them with a thin piece of wood about the size of a toothpick, careful not to get too much glue in the crack, or it would ooze out and leave an ugly mark. It would take between four and six minutes for the epoxy to set, and this stage couldn't be rushed.

Holding together the first two pieces of what would become my new old pot was deeply, unexpectedly satisfying. Holding those two pieces, waiting for them to be joined, knowing there was nothing else I could be doing in those moments, I felt I was holding a baby in my arms—just holding, with such a quiet tenderness, doing a task and being still at the same time.

"All of me" was present.

I could not have imagined that holding two pieces of broken clay together and waiting could be so deeply satisfying. Time felt full. Closer to the truth, there was no time. That same calm engulfed me as each one of the pieces was joined to make the pot whole.

155

This simple act was so full of sweetness that now, when I am feeling rushed, I try to remember the stillness of that moment. What is left to say?

When I finally held my own pieced-together pot in my hands, a circle was completed.

I looked at my bowl and saw it was beautiful.

In the past, no matter what I did or accomplished, I still felt that something was missing. When I put the pieces of my cracked pot together, I saw that *nothing* was missing.

Nothing.

I saw I was WHOLE.

That same week a letter came from a woman who had spent years living with and writing about the Shakers. In her letter I read, "The Latin root of the word 'perfect' means only 'finished,' not 'without flaws.' "

We start out whole. Complete. Along the way, we may feel that something is wrong, or missing. We aren't the way we'd like to be or the way we think we should be. A crossroads, a new stage in life, a turning point, a crisis, when we feel we may crack, or we do crack, can be a difficult, frightening time.

And, sometimes we deliberately crack our own bowl.

With time and great care and tender patience, we can reexamine the pieces, knowing that when we are ready, a solution will come. We can glue the pieces back together.

This bowl looks far more interesting, more beautiful than before it broke. The pieces are the same, but it's a different bowl than when I started.

OVERFLOWING TEA, AGAIN

More and more stories were offered, and my bowl began to feel full, even crowded. I thought again of the *Overflowing Tea* story.

"Pour me a cup of tea," the monk says, "and I will tell you when to stop." The dutiful student starts pouring the tea, and pouring and pouring the tea, and is horrified, watching as the tea spills out of the cup and over everything.

"Can't you see the cup is full?" he says. "It can hold no more!"

"And so it is with you," the wise teacher answers. "Your mind is full of too many things. Only when you are empty will there be room for more knowledge to come in."

Maybe it's time to stop—time to empty this bowl, knowing it will be filled again. Now, at the times I feel empty, I'm not as frightened as I was when I began this journey.

Being empty is a beginning.

ACCEPTANCE

When EVERYDAY SACRED first appeared in my mind's eye, I was still hoping for a *big* miracle, one that would change my life dramatically. What I found instead is the extreme importance of small things; how small miracles can make every day sacred.

Small miracles are all around us. We can find them every-where—in our homes, in our daily activities, and, hardest to see, in ourselves.

Every time I see a bowl or write a story about a bowl or make one in the studio, I hear M. C. Richards's words:

"It's not pots we are forming, it's ourselves."

Most of us are like those Zen tea bowls—uneven, cracked, imperfect. And our harsh judge keeps wishing we were perfect. The difference is the tea bowls are revered *just as they are.*

Our imperfections are a gift, the very qualities that make us unique. If we make the shift to see them that way—we can value ourselves as the monks valued those tea bowls, *just as we are.*

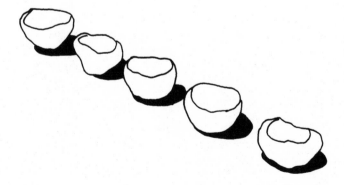

These are the teachers whose stories filled this bowl.
Together we made *Stone Soup*.

Martin Perez	Betsey Scheiner	Andrea Thompson
Helen Delfonti	Betsy Davids	Soetsu Yanagi
Ekai Korematsu	Cherie Raciti	Annie Childs
Gale Antokal	Kathleen Kelly	Dawna Mooney
Mitzi McClosky	Allan Gatzke	Wendy Palmer
Richard Bender	Leonard Koren	Jennifer Biloman
Marilyn Gordon	David Bender	Peter Steiger
Carol Field	Michael Bender	Christy Bartlett
Mel Weitsman	Joan Didion	Kevin Nierman
Audrey Tomaselli	Yvonne Rand	Robert Ryman
Nancy Webster Ware	Harriet Blanton	

ACKNOWLEDGMENTS

"Too long," the voice of the judge let me know when I started to write the *Acknowledgments*. "It sounds like an acceptance speech for the Academy Awards," Richard added. I tried to make the list leaner, but it only got longer. Finally, I decided I did not have to succeed. I did want to take the time to stop and thank each person.

So many people helped.

The list of those who are "warm in my heart" could fill another whole book.

Two people saw me through the entire process.

Mitzi McClosky's wise words, inspiration, and friendship made this book possible. Our weekly talks helped form and inform these pages.

Laurie Snowden's intelligence, creativity, keen editing talent, and dedication made an enormous contribution.

It is impossible to find enough words to say THANK YOU.

Yvonne Rand is a wise and inspiring teacher. Her wisdom can be felt throughout the manuscript. Yvonne, I am deeply grateful.

Sandy Dijkstra, my remarkable agent, offered boldness of vision, insightful suggestions, patience, and kindness.

Gale Antokal, a wonderful artist and teacher and friend, shared her ideas about art and life with an abundance of spirit. Her twins, Sam and Henry, are beloved teachers.

Laurie Fox, a friend of books, provided creative feedback and a respect for details. Kitsi Watterson's "eagle vision" when looking at a manuscript is impressive. Suzanne Lipsett offered suggestions with a fresh mind.

163

Lee Gruzen didn't put many physical marks on the manscript, but her "spirit marks" are there. She helped immensely.

Tom Grady, in the midst of his extremely busy schedule at HarperSanFrancisco, found the time to work with me again and contributed a large dose of vision.

Caroline Pincus's thoughtful, sensitive editorial suggestions and open-hearted support were a great help. Meeting her was one of the joys of this project.

Also at HarperSanFrancisco, Judy Beck is Manager of Author Relations. She is more than that. She is my dear friend and a wonderful human being. Robin Seaman brought creative imagination to our work. Cullen Curtiss and Sue White are bright, clear, and terrific at handling varied challenges. Nancy Fish and Laura Galinson are wizards at publicity. Terri Goff does copy editing with intelligence and grace.

Help comes in many forms.

A huge THANK YOU to Carol Ferraro for her rare power of seeing spirit in form.

Marilyn Gordon, Loie Rosencrantz, Jackie Wagner, Tom Cooper, and Dub Leigh saw the "bigger picture" when I was filled with doubt.

Patti Breitman, Judith Shaw, Naomi Epel, Alev Croutier, John Parman, Betsey Scheiner, Judy Goldstein, Maylie Scott, Dorothy Buckley, Joanna Taylor, Betsy Davids, and John Eberhard talked about writing. Joe Slusky, Tony Dubovsky, Jim Rosen, Robert Kulicke, Val Lavueux, Herb Bivens, Phil and Joanna Enquist, and Nancy Selvin, gifted artists, talked with me about "white" and art and design and life.

Kevin Nierman's generosity toward me was unbounded. He is a remarkable spirit and teacher, and he makes handsome cracked pots.

To M. C. Richards for inspiration.

164

The Djerassi Foundation gave a gift of silence and community.

I am grateful to Helen Delfonti for her optimism in the midst of terrible circumstances—and for reminding me, "Why waste time being unhappy?"—to Ekai Korematsu for his friendship, to Lon Addison for being a computer genius who makes house calls and for being my friend, to Nancy and Steve Selvin for their generosity, to Kathryn Miller for her artful persistence, to Martin Perez for making delicious cappuccino and doing everything with care, and to all the helpers at Cafe Milano.

Martha and Steve Rosenblatt offered the use of their trailer when I needed to get away and write. They made it easy to ask.

Robert Ryman made paintings that spoke to my soul. Thank you for saying, "Sometimes I have to go through a lot of complexity to get to simplicity."

Jill and John Walsh, Ruth and Alan Stein, Arthur and Helene Rosenfeld, Betty Bender, Kendra Peterson, Harriet Blanton, Claire Held, Judith Shaw, Junko Shisedo Cook, Angie Theirot, Martha Halperin, Ród Kiracoffe, Edith Kasin, Yvette Lehman, Marilyn Levine, Bob and Joyce Menschel, Chris and Fred Ford, John and Lois Eberhard, Jim and Morley Clark, Barbara and Jon Beckmann, and Joanna and Dan Rose all listened and helped in special ways.

Gordon Chun, an artist at book design, understood the soul of the project. He knew how to put *SPIRIT* into form. The more I work with Gordon, the more I admire him.

And finally, to Michael and David, whom I love and respect. Thank you for being fine teachers as well as wonderful sons.

The circle began with Richard and ends with Richard. "I am a saint to live with you," Richard has said. He probably is. I am forever grateful for his love, support, patience, and enormous creativity.